THE CLASSICS OF GOLF

Edition of

THE GOLF COURSES OF THE BRITISH ISLES

Text by **Bernard Darwin**

Illustrations by **Harry Rountree**

Foreword by Herbert Warren Wind

Afterword by Ben Crenshaw

Foreword

Upon his graduation from Cambridge University in 1897, Bernard Darwin made two grievous errors. In those days, many bright university graduates with no special sphere of interest embarked upon a legal career. Many of them discovered it to be stimulating and financially rewarding. Darwin became a solicitor, but he found the work dull and distant. He thought that the answer might lie in becoming a barrister. After several years of assiduous study, he passed the examinations and, in due course, was called to the Bar. He felt no more at home as a barrister than he had as a solicitor. He did not have the cast of mind that exults in the law.

In 1907, this became much more apparent to him shortly after his good friend, Arthur Croome, who wrote a weekly golf column for the London Evening Standard *and who was preparing to shift to the London* Morning Post, *recommended Darwin as a well-qualified replacement to the editors of the* Evening Standard. *Darwin's first article for the paper was about Lord Dunraven's private course near the town of Adare, in Ireland, which he had recently visited. "It had a ruined castle and an abbey as possibly attainable hazards, and I made the obvious quotation from Sir Lucius O'Trigger as to there being very snug lying in the Abbey," Darwin wrote many years later in his autobiography, "The World That Fred Made". His weekly golf column in the* Evening Standard *was so successful that the London* Times *and* Country Life, *one of the top English weekly magazines, invited him to write for them. In 1908, he left the* Evening

Standard *and accepted the offer of the* Times. *He had already begun to contribute to* Country Life *on a regular basis. Darwin had a wife and three children to take care of, but the enthusiastic reaction to his golf writing had been heartening, and he believed that golf was bound to become an increasingly popular game. "Here was richness indeed, if on a modest scale," he wrote in his autobiography, "and sometime in 1908 I sold my wig and walked out of the Temple a free man." That is a sentence that sticks with anyone who has read that excellent book.*

If Bernard Darwin became a sort of overnight sensation, he certainly had the proper credentials, apart from being a grandson of Charles Darwin, the great naturalist. (The Darwins are a remarkably gifted family.) He had an enviable education: Summerfield, a fine private school near Oxford; Eton, the famous public school; and Cambridge University. (His college was Trinity.) Growing up he had read and re-read such everlastingly beckoning novels as "Pickwick Papers", "Vanity Fair", "David Copperfield", "The Adventures of Sherlock Holmes", "Middlemarch", and "Pendennis". Darwin's erudition found its way into his golf writing, for there were many occasions in the tournaments he covered when an appropriate declaration or response by one of Dickens' small army of characters came leaping to his mind.

And Darwin knew golf. He began to play it when he was eight. He struck his first golf shot either in his grandmother's meadow in Cambridge or at Aberdovey, in Wales, where his mother's family lived. His uncle,

Arthur Ruck, had built the first rough course there, using flower pots as the cups. His father Francis, a general practitioner who chose not to practice medicine and became an internationally renowned botanist, was one of the many middle-aged Englishmen who took up golf in the 1880s. In the summers, Francis Darwin always picked a seaside resort with a good golf course for the family holiday: Felixstowe, in Suffolk, was succeeded by Cromer, in Norfolk, and by Eastbourne, on the English Channel. Darwin played a lot of golf on these courses and on the new eighteen-hole course at Aberdovey, which another uncle, Richard Ruck, had laid out. As a boy growing up in Cambridge, he had no alternative and had to put up with the primitive course on Coldham Common. The clayey soil was frequently muddy in winter, and in summer the ground became hard as a rock. In his last year at Cambridge, 1896–1897, Darwin captained the Cambridge golf team. The following year, he was one of the original members of the Oxford & Cambridge Golfing Society. He became a fine player. In 1909 and 1921, he was a semi-finalist in the British Amateur. Both times he was beaten by the eventual champion, Robert Maxwell and Willie Hunter.

In 1910, when Darwin was in his third year as the Times' golf correspondent, the London firm of Duckworth & Company brought out "The Golf Courses of the British Isles". The text was by Darwin. He had made good use of his gifts, and was already a knowledgeable, discerning, and thoroughly enjoyable writer. The book's sparkling watercolor illustrations were the work of Harry Rountree, a New Zealander, who had recently come to London. Rountree was best known as an illustrator of children's books. He was especially skillful in making the animals who were major characters in the plots come vividly to life. Darwin, I would guess, probably worked on this project chiefly in the autumn of 1909 and winter of 1910, when there were few tournaments to cover. I would guess that when Darwin discussed the project with Rountree, who was a golfer, he probably gave him a list of the courses to which he planned to devote most attention. One concludes that these two busy men decided that it would be much more practical if they did not plan to visit the courses together. In any event, in only a few instances do Rountree's paintings—and they are wonderful—delineate a particular feature of a course which Darwin describes in some detail. They dovetailed effectively on Westward Ho! Rountree painted the massive sleepered bunker, the Cape, which the golfer must carry off the tee on the fourth, a short par 4, and Darwin, in writing about the course, states, "The fourth marks our real introduction to Westward Ho! for here in front of the tee is the famous bunker we have so often heard of . . ." At Troon, Rountree elected to paint the short eighth with its "Postage Stamp" green, and Darwin begins his detailed description of the hole by declaring, "Perhaps it was the same profane person who called the eighth 'the Postage Stamp'. Certainly the green is very small, and it looks smaller than it really is as we stand trembling on the tee with some form of pitching club in hand . . ."

More often than not, however, Rountree goes his own way. At Aberdovey, for example, he does not paint the third hole, Cader, a blind one-shotter that looms large in

Darwin's memory of his cherished visits to that happy spot on the coast of Wales. Rountree really doesn't paint any part of the course. He lets us notice that the edge of a tee is in the foreground, but what has arrested his attention is a boat with white sails that rides in the blue Dovey Estuary close by the village. Soft purple hills rise in the distance beyond the harbor. Of the two paintings that Rountree did of Hoylake, the one called "Looking over to Hilbre" does not really picture that well-known hole, the twelfth, but is unabashedly a stunning view of the wide Dee Estuary at low tide. One of Rountree's two paintings evoked by Portmarnock, the splendid Irish course that lies on a thin peninsula not far from Dublin, shows four golfers huddled together in a small horse-drawn cart that is taking them across the inlet that separates the peninsula from the main body of land. At Royal Worlington, which is about seven miles from Newmarket—and which may well be the best nine-hole course in the world—Rountree set up his easel about a hundred and fifty yards from the fifth, a bunkerless par 3 that many golfers consider one of the best short holes anywhere. In his independent way, Rountree decided to paint the sixth hole, a fine par 5, on which the fairway is bordered along the right by a thick stand of fir trees. The fairway eventually darts further to the right, and the green is tucked just beyond the end of the stand of firs. It takes two big, bold shots by a long hitter to carry the firs and reach the green. Rountree's painting depicts a mustachioed golfer standing in the rough amid the trunks of the firs, about fifty yards short of the green. His hands are on his hips, and a doleful expression is on his face. He is a tall man who looks a good deal like Darwin.

The beauty of it all is that the combination of Darwin's evocative style and Rountree's fetching watercolors works out wondrously well. In a way, what with its ample illustrations, "The Golf Courses of the British Isles" must have been one of the earliest coffee-table books. In another way, since that term is now generally used to describe gift books that are short on content, large in size, printed on glossy paper, prolifically illustrated, high priced, and meant to occupy an obvious position on a key table in the owner's parlor, "The Golf Courses of the British Isles" is the very antithesis of a coffee-table book. Rather, it is the kind of book which British golfers and golfers around the globe have gone back to frequently to re-read what Darwin had to say about a particular course. On its publication, the book enjoyed a brisk and healthy sale, and it earned a place long ago among the authentic classics of golf.

This reprinting of "The Golf Courses of the British Isles" is the inspiration of Robert Macdonald, the publisher of The Classics of Golf. A man of creative bent who has a strong background in golf and the arts, Macdonald came to the conclusion that this was an appropriate time to make this watershed book once more available to the game's devotees. Copies of the original edition are hard to come by these days, and, moreover, they have continued to rise in value and now command a very high price. There are only a few copies available of a revised edition, "The Golf Courses of Great Britain", which was published in 1925 by Jonathan Cape Ltd. For that edition, Darwin went to the considerable work of bringing up to date the alterations made in the courses he describes, and he also added his views on prominent new courses that had come into existence. In his preface to the revised edition, Darwin explains why the chapter on the golf courses of Ireland had to be omitted: "It is so long since I have played on them that I felt it impossible to write about them accurately, and so have thought it better not to write at all. I am the more sorry because it is on Irish courses that I have spent some of the pleasantest days of a golfing life."

Arranging for the publication of this new edition of "The Golf Courses of the British Isles" was no simple undertaking for Macdonald. For example, the color separations for reproducing Rountree's watercolors were done in Singapore. After studying Rountree's work, Macdonald came to some interesting conclusions. He believes that after Rountree had painted the huge bunker on the fourth hole at Westward Ho!, he might have decided then and there to do no more paintings that focussed on a single bunker regardless of the bunker's distinguished place in golf history. Macdonald is also of the opinion that, as Rountree began to move from course to course on his fascinating assignment, early on he came to a definite decision: each painting would be different; he would not repeat a composition. Macdonald further believes that whenever there was water on or near a golf course—the ocean, the sea, an estuary, a river, a stream, a burn, or a pond—Rountree was irresistibly drawn to it. Rountree was a golfer who loved golf, but, as is especially apparent in such paintings as "On Gullane Hill" and "St. Andrews: the town from the distance", the correct rendering of an historic hole, a celebrated green, or a renowned hazard was not his primary consideration.

Ben Crenshaw has kindly provided the Afterword for this selection. He is the right man. In addition to being a golfer of distinction, he is a golf-course architect and a true Darwin scholar. On the walls of the dining room of his house in Austin are a few original Rountree paintings: one oil and two watercolors.

Herbert Warren Wind

*Facsimile of the 1910
edition published in
London by Duckworth & Co.*

ST. ANDREWS

Looking back from the twelfth green

THE GOLF COURSES

OF THE

BRITISH ISLES

BY

BERNARD DARWIN

ILLUSTRATED BY

HARRY ROUNTREE

LONDON

DUCKWORTH & CO.

3 HENRIETTA STREET, COVENT GARDEN

CONTENTS

LIST OF ILLUSTRATIONS

LIST OF ILLUSTRATIONS

CHAPTER I.

LONDON COURSES (1).

SOME dozen or fifteen years ago the historian of the London golf courses would have had a comparatively easy task. He would have said that there were a few courses upon public commons, instancing, as he still would to-day, Blackheath and Wimbledon. He might have dismissed in a line or two a course that a few mad barristers were trying to carve by main force out of a swamp thickly covered with gorse and heather near Woking. All the other courses would have been lumped together under some such description as that they consisted of fields interspersed by trees and artificial ramparts, the latter mostly built by Tom Dunn; that they were villainously muddy in winter, of an impossible and adamantine hardness in summer, and just endurable in spring and autumn; finally, that the muddiest and hardest and most distinguished of them all was Tooting Bec.

All this is changed now, and the change is best exemplified by the fact that although the club has removed to new quarters, poor Tooting itself is now as Tadmor in the

A   1

wilderness. I passed by the spot the other day, and should never have recognized it had not an old member pointed it out to me in a voice husky with emotion. The ground is now covered with a tangle of red houses, which cannot be termed attractive, and such glory as belonged to it has altogether departed. Peace to its ashes! it could never, by the wildest stretch of imagination, have been called anything but a bad course, and yet it held its head high in its heyday. Prospective members by the score jostled each other eagerly on the waiting list, and parliamentary golfers distinguished the course above its fellows by cutting their divots from its soft and yielding mud. I still recollect the thrill I experienced on first being taken to play there; it was a distinct moment in my golfing life. It was exceedingly muddy, but it was not so muddy as the course at Cambridge on which I usually disported myself, and on the whole I thought it worthy of its fame; people were not so difficult to please in the matter of inland golf in those days.

Tooting is no more, but there are many courses like it still to be found, most of them in a flourishing condition, near London. Meanwhile, however, a new star, the star of sand and heather, has arisen out of the darkness, and a whole generation of new courses, which really are golf and not a good or even bad imitation of it, have sprung into being. Here are some of them, and they make an imposing list—Sunningdale, Walton Heath, Woking, Worplesdon, Byfleet, Bleakdown, Westhill, Bramshot and Combe Wood. The idea of hacking and digging and building a course out of land on which two blades of grass do not originally grow together is a comparatively modern one. The elder 'architects' took a piece of country that was more or less ready to their hand, rolled it and mowed it, cut some trenches and built some ramparts, and there was the course. They did not as a rule think of taking a primaeval pine forest or a waste of heather and forcibly turning it into a course; if they had thought of it, moreover, they would not have had the money to carry it out. Now the glorious golfing properties of this country of sand and heather and fir-trees have been discovered; its owners too have discovered that they possessed all unknowingly a gold mine from which can be extracted so many hundreds of pounds an acre, and the work of building courses out of the heather and building houses all round it goes gaily on.

These heathery courses are, for the most part, very good, and so indeed they ought to be. They have, in the first place, the priceless gift of youth. Those who have laid them out have been able to study both the merits and the faults of the older courses, and then, with the advantage of all this accumulated mass of knowledge, have set themselves to the work of creation. This science, for so it may now be fairly called, of the laying out of courses on carefully discussed and thought-out principles, is itself comparatively modern; the very expression 'a good length hole,' which is now upon all golfers' lips, is of no great antiquity. Those who laid out the older links did not, one may hazard the opinion, think a vast deal about the good or bad length

3

of their hole. They saw a plateau which nature had clearly intended for a green, and another plateau at some distance off which had the appearance of a tee, and there was the hole ready made for them; whether the distance from one plateau to another could be compassed in a drive and a pitch, or in two drives, or perhaps even two drives and a pitch, did not, I fancy, greatly interest them. In some places nature, being in a particularly kindly mood, had disposed the plateaus at ideal distances, so that a St. Andrews sprang into being; but people as a rule took the holes as they found them, and were not for ever searching for the perfect ' test of golf.'

Gradually, however, the more thoughtful of golfers evolved definite theories as to what were the particular qualities that constituted a good or bad hole, and longed for an opportunity of putting their theories into practice. One such great opportunity came when it was discovered that heather would, if only enough money was spent on it, make admirable golfing country, and the architects have made the fullest use of it, lavishing upon the heather treasures of thought, care and ingenuity which the non-golfer might say were worthy of a better cause. Nothing can ever quite make up for the short, crisp turf, the big sandhills and the smell of the sea; seaside golf must always come first, and inland second, but the best inland golf can no longer be reproached with being a bad second.

Of all these comparatively young courses, the two best known are probably Sunningdale and Walton Heath. **Sunningdale** was designed by Willy Park, who is an

SUNNINGDALE

The tenth hole

architect of very pronounced characteristics, though Sunningdale is not perhaps quite so clearly to be recognized as his handiwork as are some of his other courses, such as Huntercombe or Burhill. It was laid out in what proved to be the last days of the gutty ball, though there was then no whisper of the revolution that was coming to us across the Atlantic. It was a long course—really a fearfully long course for an ordinary mortal. The two-shot holes were doubtless two-shot holes—for Braid, but they had a way of expanding themselves into two drives and a reasonable iron shot for less gifted players. I cannot help thinking that the coming of the 'Haskell' was a blessing for the course, and that it may be said of Sunningdale, as it can be said for perhaps no other course in Christendom, that it was improved by the rubber-cored ball.

The holes are still quite long enough, and if we accomplish any considerable number of them in four strokes apiece we shall be justified in a modified amount of swagger, but we need no longer risk an internal injury in trying to reach the green with our second shot. Of all the inland courses Sunningdale is perhaps the richest in really fine two-shot holes, where a brassey or cleek shot lashed right home on to the green sends a glow of satisfaction through the golfer's frame.

Almost as surely as the two-shot holes constitute its strength, the short holes are the weakness of the course. Really good and interesting short holes add a crowning glory to a golf course, and that, I think, Sunningdale lacks.

5

GOLF COURSES

It resembles in that respect another fine course, Deal, where the longer holes are admirable and the short holes are almost totally wanting in distinction. The short holes at Sunningdale are, however, much better than they used to be, for there was a time when they might have been rather scathingly dismissed as consisting of two practically blind shots on to artificial table lands, and a third entirely blind shot on to a bad sloping green; but this third reproach at least has now been entirely wiped away.

Let us now begin at the first tee and duly admire the view over a vast expanse of wild, undulating, heathery country, with more houses on it now than anyone except the ground-landlord would like to see, and clumps of fir-trees here and there, one especially on a little knoll, which makes a pleasant landmark in the distance. The next thing to do is to hit the ball, which should be a comparatively easy task, for there is plenty of room at this first hole, as there always should be, and nothing but an egregious top or a wholly unprovoked slice is likely to harm us. It is really, from the point of view of the greatest happiness of the greatest number, a wholly admirable first hole, since not only is there no great opportunity for disaster, but the hole is a long hole and so enables the couples to be despatched quickly and without undue irritation from the tee. It is just a steady, easy-going five hole—two drives and a pitch—a mere prelude to the beginning of serious business at the second.

This second is a really good hole. The tee-shot has to be played at an unpleasantly difficult angle, and if we slice

6

LONDON

it we may find ourselves in some innocent householder's front garden, while in endeavouring to avoid such a trespass, we shall most probably pull it into a region of ruts and heather. If we avoid both forms of errors, we have still the second shot to play, long and straight and of an aspect most formidable, for the avenue of rough down which we drive narrows as it approaches the green, and there is an indefinable temptation to slice. Altogether a fine hole, and on the easiest of days we may be thoroughly pleased with a four, a figure we ought to repeat at the third. This third is of no vast length, but is an excellent example of those holes whereat there is much virtue in the placing of the tee-shot. There is a bunker that "pokes and nuzzles with its nose" into the left-hand or top edge of the green, and he who pulls his drive ever so slightly will have a most difficult pitch to play over this bunker on to a somewhat slippery and sloping green that runs away from him. On the other hand, the man who has had the courage to skirt the rough on the right-hand side of the course—very bad rough it is, too—will be rewarded by a fairly simple run up shot, and moreover, the slope of the green makes a cushion against which he may play his shot boldly.

The fourth is a short hole on a plateau green some way above the player. The plateau is reasonably small and well guarded, and the shot in a cross wind is sufficiently difficult, but the bottom of the pin is out of the player's sight, and he needs much local knowledge to be sure whether he is ten yards short or stone dead; a better hole

7

than it was, maybe, but not quite worthy of Sunningdale yet.

The fifth and sixth are beautiful holes, and the tee-shot to the fifth sends the blood coursing more briskly through the veins. There is an exhilaration in driving from a height and rushing thence down a steep place on to the course which cannot be gainsaid. The more scientific may point out that there is no justification for such emotion and that we have far less on which to plume ourselves than if we had struck our tee-shot from the flat. The fact remains that hitting off a high place, if it be not done too often and we are not too scant of breath, is wholly delightful; the difficulty is that we are so intoxicated with the situation that we hit much too hard and the ball totters feebly down the hill-side, suffering from a severe wound in the scalp.

The drive from this particular high place having been safely accomplished, there is an accurate second shot, which varies greatly in length according to the wind, to be played between a pond on the right and a bunker on the left. Some will pitch it and pitch into the pond; others will run it and run into the bunker, and Mr. Colt will play a peculiar low, scuffling shot straight on the pin and win it from us in a four, which will very nearly be a three. Another wonderfully good two-shot hole is the sixth, where the green lies in the angle of a wood, and we must hold our second shot well up to the left so that the ball shall trickle slowly down the sloping green towards the hole; that is supposing we have hit a straight tee-shot, a thing by no means certain, for there is a horribly attractive clump of fir-trees to the left which catches many and which once proved particularly fatal to Jack White in a big match against Tom Vardon.

The seventh is a bone of contention, some averring that it is a fine 'sporting' hole, while others have no names too bad for it; when not alluded to with profanity it is generally known as the 'Switch-back' hole. Those who like a blind tee-shot and a blind second will admire it, and those who don't wont, and there is the whole matter in a very small compass. The eighth is quite a good short hole now (it used to be bad and blind and stupid); and the ninth we may skip, although there is a fine straight tee-shot needed, and then from the tenth tee we drive down another steep place into the lower country. Those who make a loud outcry when they drive "a perfect tee-shot, sir, straight on the pin," and find it in a bunker, may here have cause for annoyance. There is no bunker on the straight line, but there are bunkers to right and left and a somewhat narrow space between, and a shot that is very, very nearly well hit sometimes finds a resting-place in one or other of them. It is a poor thing, however, to demand perfect immunity for any respectable drive, and the shot that is placed where it ought to be gives the chance for a really fine second shot between more bunkers on to a green of fascinating but fiendish undulations. At the back of the green is a hut, where live ginger-beer and apples and other things, and he who has done the hole in four fully deserves them. This tenth hole will be celebrated in golfing history for a truly tremendous second shot played

by Braid out of the left-hand bunker in the final round
of the *News of the World* tournament, his opponent being
Edward Ray. Braid calls it in his book the most remarkable bunker shot that he ever played, and that is praise
indeed. Poor Ray! He had a perfect tee-shot and a
perfect second, laid his third stone dead, and yet lost the
hole, for Braid, having driven into the left-hand bunker
from the tee, gallantly took his iron for his second, reached
the green with a terrific shot, and completed the roll of
his infamies by holing his putt for a three.

Provided we do not top our tee-shot into a formidable
sandy bluff, the eleventh should be done in four, with a
chance of a three; and the twelfth should be another four,
if only we can be straight enough from the tee. This is
a hole to be approached warily and in instalments, and
the prudent man generally takes a cleek or a spoon from
the tee, and even then breathes a fervent thanksgiving if
his ball lies clear, since the fairway narrows down to a
horribly small point.

The thirteenth, as I said, was once one of the very worst
holes in the world, and is now a thoroughly attractive one;
the player must produce some stroke whereby the ball
shall sit resolutely down on a slanting green surrounded
by bunkers, and stay there. The fourteenth is a two-shot
hole for Mr. Angus Hambro, and rather more for most
other people, save under favourable conditions. Then
comes another short hole—I should have said there were
four and not three—but this is a long short hole; a wooden
club shot is often needed, and when that wooden club shot

10

has to be held up into a stiff right-hand wind, the difficulties of the situation are not easily to be overrated.

Then we face homewards with three good long holes, all of which may be done in fours, though most people would thankfully strike a bargain with Providence for two fours and a five. The most difficult of the three, as is only right and fitting, is a seventeenth hole, and here Mr. Colt has worked a great transformation and turned a hole that once possessed no merits whatever into a thoroughly good one, with a most difficult second shot—one of those shots which produce an instinctive and fatal tendency to slice. After that two good, straight, steady shots should get us safely on to the home green, and we have finished at last; if we have done a score which is perceptibly lower than 80, we have done well. If we have not been too frequently 'up to our necks' in untrodden heather—nay, even if we have—we ought to have enjoyed ourselves immensely.

From Sunningdale we go to **Walton Heath**—a thing far easier to accomplish in the imagination than by a cross-country journey, and there we have another fine, long slashing course laid out in the grand manner, especially to suit the rubber-cored ball.

The course is the work of Mr. Herbert Fowler, who is perhaps the most daring and original of all golfing architects, and gifted with an almost inspired eye for the possibilities of a golfing country. He is essentially ferocious in his methods, and there is no one else who is quite so merciless in the punishing of shots that are quite respectable, that are in fact so nearly good that the striker of

11

them, in the irritation of the moment, calls them perfect. This fell design he will accomplish either by trapping the long shot that is almost straight but not straight enough or by planting his green amid a perfect network of bunkers. The result is that there will always be found some to call down maledictions upon his head, and in truth some of his devices are almost fiendish, but they are nearly always interesting.

The trend of modern golfing architecture is all against the old-fashioned cross-bunkers, which used as a matter of course to be dug at regular intervals across the fairway, but, curiously enough, the cross-bunker plays a not unimportant part at Walton. Two holes in particular come to mind, the long seventh and eighth, where bunkers have to be crossed and cannot be circumvented, while the crossing of them in the proper number of strokes is a very essential matter, since the necessity of playing short often involves the loss of a whole stroke.

Wild and bleak and merciless the course looks—a vast tract of wind-swept heather. In truth it is a very long one, and the casual visitor often brings against it a charge of monotonous length, but when he has played there more often he will probably discover that each of these long holes has a very distinct character, and that each is interesting in a way of its own. Some courses impress themselves very quickly on the memory so that each hole stands out quite distinctly, while others leave only a vague and blurred recollection, nor is it merely a question of the holes being absolutely good or bad. When a man has once played the

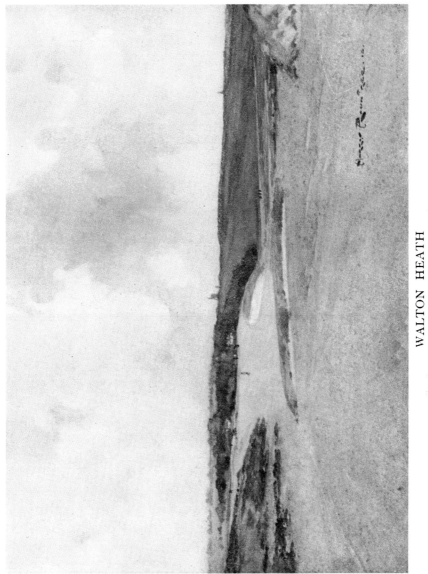

WALTON HEATH

The second shot at the seventeenth hole

first six holes at Sandwich he is likely to remember them all the days of his life, even if he has avoided the Sahara and the Maiden; whereas he may retain only the haziest recollection of St. Andrews after two or three days' play. So it is with the long holes at Walton Heath; they have in reality plenty of character, but it is hard at first to distinguish one from another.

The short holes, on the other hand, make a vivid and lasting impression, and, as I think at least, give to the course its chief distinction. There are four of them, and all four are good. Of these four the sixth is by common consent the best and most difficult; so difficult as sometimes to be paid the high compliment of being called 'impossible.' When the professionals were playing at Walton in the *News of the World* tournament, and playing with their wonderful and monotonous accuracy—shot after shot clean, long, and straight as an arrow through the wind—it was pleasant to find that there existed in the world quite a short hole which could show them to be vulnerable. I stood on the first day watching a succession of couples play this sixth hole, and though there was usually one ball safely on the green, there were never two; it was really a most cheering and satisfactory spectacle.

Even on the stillest of still days the shot is one which can scarce be approached without a tremor. The distance can be compassed with a firm pitch with an iron club of moderate loft, and the green is undeniably of adequate size, but it is ringed round, save immediately in front, with a series of bunkers very deep and horrible, and, to increase

13

our terror, the ground 'draws' unmistakably towards them. Often as we stand on the tee in a frenzied attitude, trying to steer the ball to safety with vain gesticulations of the club, we see it light upon the turf, and breathe a sigh of relief. Alas, we were too hasty! The ball trembles and totters for a moment or two, in a state of indecision, and then, as if magnetically drawn towards Scylla on one side or Charybdis on the other, slowly disappears from our sight. Once in the bunker there is nothing to do but employ the 'common thud' of Sir Walter Simpson, and we ought with ordinary fortune to get out in one, but the ball must be made to drop wonderfully dead and lifeless, scattering showers of sand as it goes, or else it will run quite gently and deliberately across the green into the bunker on the other side. It is one of those holes at which, were the fates amenable to a compromise, many a stout-hearted player would write down four on his card and proceed to the next tee with the ball in his pocket.

Another hole of similar character, but a degree or two less formidable and by just so much the less fascinating, is the twelfth. Perhaps it would be just as terrible were it not that the prevailing wind is here behind the player, whereas at the sixth it seems to blow persistently across. With the wind behind the hole is brought within the compass of an ordinary, straightforward, inartistic thump with a mashie, and that shot, which is the *bête noire* of all but the truly great, the push with the iron, is not brought into requisition.

The other two short holes, the fifth and the tenth, are

never very short, and, when the wind blows strong in our faces, too long for us to entertain any great hopes of reaching the green. In any case, unless the ground be abnormally hard and fast, we had better behave with due humility and take a wooden club. At the fifth our chief care must be to hold the ball well up to the right, a task usually made more difficult by a strong pulling wind. There are many chronic and many occasional slicers in the world, but there are few who can deliberately hit the ball to the right and make it hold on its way when they want to : wonderfully few who can do so without a disastrous loss of distance. It is the chief beauty of the hole that it calls imperatively for this most difficult of shots, since the slope of the green is from right to left and a series of graduated horrors await the pulled ball : a mere bunker for the moderate sinner, a tract of wet ruts and hoof-marks for the rather more criminal, and a waste of heather for the utterly depraved. Nor is it sufficient merely to hit the ball somewhere out to the right. Good intentions by themselves are not enough, and there is a bunker lurking on the right-hand edge of the green ; if we go so far to the right that this bunker lies between us and the hole, we shall have to employ all the arts of a Taylor if we are to be within reasonable putting range next time.

Now we must leave the tenth, though an excellent hole, especially as played by Braid with a vast, low skimming cleek shot, and look at some of the longer holes. Of these there are three which fix themselves in the memory, the second, seventeenth and eighteenth. A hole more satisfactory to do in four than the second it would be hard to imagine, since both the drive and the second must be long and straight and the second must almost inevitably be played from a hanging lie. We may, if we like, approach it in cowardly instalments and play our tee-shot deliberately short of the sloping ground; if we do, we may possibly escape a six, but by no means shall we get a four. It is the hole for a man brave and skilful who can use his wooden club when the ground is not flat, neither is the ball teed.

It is the duty of every golf course to have a good seventeenth hole, and the seventeenth at Walton certainly need not fear comparison even with the Alps and the Stationmaster's Garden. We must begin by hitting a long, straight drive between bunkers on the right and some particularly retentive heather on the left, but that is, comparatively speaking, an easy matter. The second shot is the thing—a full shot right home on to a flat green that crowns the top of a sloping bank. To the right the face of the hill is excavated in a deep and terrible bunker, and a ball ever so slightly sliced will run into that bunker as sure as fate. To the left there is heather extending almost to the edge of the green, and, in avoiding the right-hand bunker, we may very likely die an even more painful death in the heather.

After this glorious hole the eighteenth seems simple enough. Two lusty, straightforward drives, with a big bunker to carry for the second; it is a hole that presents few terrors to the professional, since he always hits his wooden club shots, yet even for him there are some bunkers at the edge of the green which are not to be despised. For humbler people everything connected with the hole is very far from despicable.

Besides the greens, which are big and true and fraught with undulations difficult to gauge, there is one feature which calls for special mention, and that is the deepness of the bunkers. It is part of Mr. Fowler's ferocity that he does not intend us to run through his bunkers, if he can by any means prevent it, while, when we are in them, he does not mean us to do more than get out with a niblick. Braid can sometimes hit prodigious distances out of them, but then he has been round the course in a score under 70—a thing that no respectable man should do.

Before quitting the heathery courses, we must take a glance at **Woking,** which is the oldest and still one of the best of them. Indeed, although my judgment may not be strictly an impartial one, I think it is still the pleasantest of all upon which to play, and the golf is undeniably interesting. It does lack something, however, of the big-ness of Sunningdale or Walton Heath, which have been laid out on an altogether grander scale. The two-shot holes at Woking do not always require quite two shots. When the ground is at all hard a poorish drive does not do a great deal of harm, and a long one means a comfortable second shot with an iron club. Still, continuous brassey play is not everything : it is apt to grow monotonous, and whatever charge can be made against Woking, I imagine that no just critic would call it dull. The keenest golfer among my acquaintances said to me the other day that, whatever anybody might say, Sandwich and Woking were the two pleasantest places for a game of golf, and though there is no resemblance between the two courses, I think his verdict was a sound one.

Woking has certain, almost unique, distinctions—or disgraces, according to one's point of view—among golf clubs. It has but one medal day a year, and it possesses no Bogey. Any innocent stranger visiting Woking and enquiring the bogey score for any particular hole will be greeted with a glare of such withering contempt as seriously to impair his day's pleasure. Another curious, and I think a blessed, circumstance about Woking is that the bunkers, which are many and cunningly disposed, are the work of one benevolent autocrat. Unconscious of their doom, the members disperse for their summer holidays and when they return they find that the most revolutionary things have been done. Upon greens that were formerly flat and easy have sprouted plateaus and domes and hollows. Hillocks have risen as if by magic in the middle of the fairway; 'floral' hazards bloom at the side, and bunkers have been dug at that precise spot where members have for years complacently watched their ball come to rest at the end of their finest shots. Even now as I write I believe there is a gigantic project in view at a certain hole, which I would rather die than reveal. All these things happen at the instigation of a very small secret Junta, and after a little grumbling, such as is only right and proper, the members settle down and admit that the alterations are exceedingly ingenious and the course more entertaining than ever. It appears

18

WOKING

Looking back to the sixteenth green

to me to be the ideal way in which to conduct a golf club, but it is an ideal that can very seldom be attained.

Over one of the revolutionary things done at Woking controversy still rages, or rather it no longer continuously rages, but spirts every now and again into flame. This is the famous bunker at the fourth hole, of which the traveller may get a fine view as he is being whirled towards Southampton by the South-Western Railway. This hole was originally a very ordinary 'drive and a pitch' hole. You drove straight down a fairly broad strip of turf between heather on the left and the railway line on the right. Then you jumped over a rampart on to a nice big green and there you were. The soul of Mr. Stuart Paton, however, soared far above so lamentably unimaginative a hole, and he set to work upon it. First he removed large portions of the cross-rampart, so that it became possible to play a running instead of a pitching shot from certain positions, and then in the very centre of the fairway, at just the range of a good drive from the tee, he dug a small but formidable bunker. In shape it bore a resemblance to the Principal's Nose, while in position it was rather like that of the bunker which lies in the middle of the course going to the ninth hole also at St. Andrews. By means of this bunker a clear-cut and distinct problem has to be faced on the tee. We must decide whether to drive safely away to the left, and so have a pitch to play, which is sometimes rather difficult, or whether to take a risk and lay down the ball between the bunker and the railway line. The danger of pushing the ball out a little too much, and so going out of bounds, is considerable, but the reward is considerable also, for an easy running up shot should give us a putt for three.

The number of discussions which I have heard as to this one little bunker would fill a large but not an interesting volume. The form of the discussion is nearly always the same, and is something like this :

 A. "You can't persuade me that it is right to have a bunker bang on the line to the hole, exactly where a good drive should be."

 B. "If there is a bunker there, then that cannot be the line to the hole. Your drive was not a very good one, but a very bad one."

 A. "It was not a bad one. It was a perfect shot—hit in the very middle of the club."

 B. "You should use your own head as well as the club head."

After this the conversation becomes unfit for publication.

There are also some bunkers situated actually in the putting greens which used to cause annoyance. There is one at the sixth and two at the seventeenth, one of which is affectionately called "Johnny Low," after that sternest of bunker-makers, who invented it. To these, however, everybody has long been reconciled, and both holes afford good instances of how much can be done in the way of making a player place his tee-shot, by digging a comparatively small bunker in the green.

Another clever and interesting piece of golfing architecture is to be found at the seventh hole. The hole can be reached from the tee with a moderate iron shot, and in former days, so long as one did not slice or pull very egregiously, one could recover from a most indifferent shot by laying a long putt dead on a flat easy green. Now, however, a most ingenious range of mountains has been introduced, which has had the effect of dividing the green into two compartments. If a shot be at all crooked a three is still well within the bounds of possibility, but the approach putt, instead of being easy, has to be made over a series of most perplexing curves. The straight player's ball, on the other hand, is lying close to the hole, for the hills, which are the enemies of the crooked, are as a rule the allies of the accurate, and have rewarded his virtuous ball with a kick from their friendly slopes. A somewhat similar architectural feat has been tried at the other short hole—the sixteenth, where we have to pitch over a pond— but there, for some reason, it hardly seems to have been so successful.

I am afraid I may have given the idea that Woking has been laid out in a spirit of impish mischief, but such an impression would be an entirely wrong one. There are plenty of opportunities for fine, straightforward hitting, although wild, erratic slogging will nearly always be punished. There are some really beautiful two-shot holes, which are at their best when there is not too much run in the ground. The fifth, for instance, where there is a wonderfully pretty green lying in a semi-circle of trees, and the eighth, a really gorgeous hole when there is any wind against one. Twelve and thirteen again, though not quite so long, are both beautiful holes, and the fourteenth, which brings the golfer right up to the club-house and tempts him to lunch before his time, requires two of the very longest and straightest of hits.

Taking them day in and day out I think the greens at Woking are the best that I know to be found inland—Mid-Surrey excepted. They are often very nearly perfect, and are practically always good. They are not as a rule alarmingly fast, nor so slow as to convert putting into mere hard physical exercise, but of a nice, easy, comfortable pace, that reflects enormous credit on Martin, who is one of the best of green-keepers. I can only end as I began by asserting that there is no more delightful course whereon to play golf.

CHAPTER II.

LONDON COURSES (2).

Now leaving the heather, we must turn to some of the other substances upon which Londoners play their weekly golf. On the course of the Mid-Surrey Golf Club in the Old Deer Park at Richmond there are probably more rounds of golf played throughout the whole year than on any other golf course in the three kingdoms. You may go down to Richmond on any day of the year, on which it is not snowing, and be sure of finding a good many people who have managed to get a day off and are spending it in playing golf. The business of the world presumably goes on in spite of their absence, and indeed the week-day crowd on a golf course points the moral that we are none of us indispensable.

The **Mid-Surrey** course is in a park, and must therefore be classed among the park courses, but it is hardly typical of its kind. The trees stand for the most part as occasional and isolated sentinels guarding the edges of the rough. We do not drive down whole avenues of them, nor, as on some courses, do they play the part of gigantic goal-posts through which we must direct the ball. The country is more open and more sparsely timbered than the typical park, but, if the big trees only interfere with us now and then, there are several peculiarly odious little spinneys which are almost certain to thrust themselves upon our notice.

The Old Deer Park is a pretty spot, but the course does not at first sight look attractive; its disadvantages may be summed up in two adjectives—'flat' and 'artificial,' nor do the course's enemies forget to make the fullest use of them. Flat it is—as flat as a pancake, as may be seen at a glance, and the bunkers, which are now innumerable as the sands of the sea, have been raised one and all by the hand of man. So much is certain, and on such a course there is a limit to our powers of enjoying ourselves; we cannot hope for the exhilaration that is born of sea and sandhills and, in a minor degree, of fir-trees and heath. On the other hand, of the joy that comes from a well-struck brassey shot—a joy that has been sadly diminished on most courses by the rubber-cored ball—we can taste in abundance. The last nine holes in the Old Deer Park repay really long straight play with the wooden clubs almost as well as any nine holes that can be mentioned, wherefore the Mid-Surrey course, if it be not quite 'the real thing' itself, provides at least an admirable training ground.

There is but one thing lacking for the player's perfect education in brassey shots, and that is an occasional bad lie or bad stance; he will constantly be taking his wooden club through the green, but the ball will always be sitting

24

MID-SURREY

The tenth hole

up on a perfect lie and obviously requesting to be hit, while his stance will be of the smoothest and flattest. When he leaves this smooth and shaven Paradise and fights the sea breezes amid hummocks and hollows, he will find that considerably more is asked of him, and may possibly re-echo the dictum of the celebrated Scottish professional, that it is necessary to be a goat in order to stand to his ball, and a goat, moreover, qualified with no uncertain epithet.

In this matter of perfect lies and stances Mid-Surrey is apt to pamper and over-indulge its devotees; and the same may be said of the greens, for they are as near perfection as anything short of a billiard-table could possibly be. Much care and money and a transcendent genius among green-keepers, Peter Lees, have combined to make them a miracle of trueness and smoothness. Some greens that are extraordinarily good, true and easy, yet afford no particular pleasure, since they are too slow and soft; a perfectly true Turkey carpet might lead to the holing of many putts and yet the player would soon long for some barer, harder, more untrue substance. The necessity of hitting our putts very hard covers many little deficiencies in our execution, but it is poor fun compared with the art of stroking the ball up to the hole.

The Mid-Surrey greens are open to none of these re-proaches, since they combine perfect trueness with plenty of pace, and we must strike the ball a delicate, subtle blow; the methods of the bludgeon are equally unsuitable and disastrous. There are plenty of little ripples and ridges

25

and hollows in the greens, though few bold slopes, and there is therefore scope for considerable nicety of putting; above all, there is the cheering knowledge that a putt has but to make a good start in life to ensure its turning neither to the right nor to the left and ending a blameless career at the bottom of the hole.

Thus we have perfect lies, stances, and greens, and it is clear that we shall have none but the most futile excuses for our errors. If we hit the ball we ought to do a good score, and, especially on the way out, nothing but our own folly should prevent a long and gratifying sequence of fours; that is to say, we ought to do six fours, two threes at the short holes, and a five, which we may fairly allow ourselves at the second. This green can be reached in two shots; Robson did reach it in two in the *News of the World* tournament, but to have seen him do it was enough to prevent our own vaulting ambition from o'erleaping itself once and for all. They were indeed two stupendous shots, and if we carry the big cross-bunker safely in two and then play a nice straight run-up on to the green, we shall have done all that can be reasonably expected of us. Of the other holes on the way out the third is perhaps the most engaging, since we must employ our heads as well as our clubs. There is a spinney—a detestably, almost mesmerically attractive spinney—to the left, and if we pull our drive we shall be confronted with a shot wherein the ball must rise abruptly to a considerable height and at the same time traverse a considerable distance. If, however, we have pushed the tee-shot well out to the right, we shall have our reward in a simple approach shot, a steady four and a consciousness of virtue.

As far as the turn, then, we may progress in an average of fours, but we shall be lucky if we do not considerably exceed it on the way home; we shall need a series of lusty second shots and even so shall be none the worse for a wind behind us at all the holes, which is alas! impossible. There is no one hole that stands out particularly from its fellows, but the one we are likely to remember best is the twelfth, not so much for its intrinsic merits, which are considerable, as for a fine cedar tree, which fills us with joy till it has entirely and hopelessly stymied us from the hole.

The bunkers are many and cunningly devised, and there is also rough grass, but the lies in the rough are not very bad, and if we are going to make a mistake we shall be well advised to do it thoroughly; thereby we shall be so crooked as to avoid the bunkers, while brute force and a driving iron may extricate us from the rough with but little loss. This, of course, is not as it should be, but the difficulty is an insuperable one on many inland courses.

Not far off are two nice courses, Sudbrook Park and Ashford Manor, but from Mid-Surrey we will voyage to another park course, the newest of its kind, at **Stoke Poges.** Stoke Park is a beautiful spot, and there is very good golf to be played there; the club is an interesting one, moreover, as being one of the first and the most ambitious attempts in England at what is called in America a 'Country Club.' There are plenty of things to do at

GOLF COURSES

Stoke besides playing golf. We may get very hot at lawn tennis or keep comparatively cool at bowls or croquet, or, coolest of all, we may sit on the terrace or in the garden and give ourselves wholly and solely to loafing. The club-house is a gorgeous palace, a dazzling vision of white stone, of steps and terraces and cupolas, with a lake in front and imposing trees in every direction, while over it all broods the great Chief-Justice Coke, looking down benignantly from the top of his pillar and gracefully concealing his astonishment at the changes in the park.

Never was there a better instance of the art of forcibly turning a forest into a golf-course than is to be found at Stoke Poges. The beautiful old park turf was always there, cropped from time immemorial by generations of deer, who little knew what service they were doing to the green-keeper, but in every direction there stretched thick belts of woodland, and yet a golf course was going to be made and opened in less than no time. I saw the place in its pristine state, and the holes, as they were pointed out to me, with an eye of but imperfect faith. Thousands of trees, as it seemed, bore the fatal mark that signified their doom, and yet the thing appeared almost impossible. One hole was particularly impressive. All that was then to be seen was a pretty little brook running innocently between its banks, which were thickly covered with trees, while on one side the ground sloped gently upwards to a path through the woods. It was a spot to conjure up visions of dryads or fairies, "Green jacket, red cap and white owl's feather"; of anything in the world except a narrow,

STOKE POGES

The sixteenth hole

catchy, slanting green and a half-iron shot. Yet an inspired architect had fixed on it as the site of one of his short holes; the trees were to be cut down, the sloping bank was to be turfed and the brook promoted to the fuller dignity of a burn. I went my way full of admiration—and of doubt.

A few months after I returned to find that the romantic little wood had vanished, and there was a short hole in its place—a hole that any course might be proud to own, and a putting green that the deer might have grazed for centuries. I never saw a more daring bit of architecture, except perhaps at Stonham, the new course near Southampton, where Willy Park has actually built a putting green over a stream. Apart from this one hole, belts of wood had disappeared in all directions as if by magic, and had been replaced by turf; yet there were so many trees left that no one could reasonably complain. There was the course ready to be played on, and a very good course it is—long, difficult, and for the most part entertaining.

The turf is good and springy, and where it is intended that the player should get a good lie, he gets an excellent one; where it is intended that he should be in trouble there is likewise no mistake about it. He may lie in a wood, though this is only the penalty for a very heinous crime, and the trees are for the most part kept skilfully in reserve as a second line of defence. He may at one or two holes lie in a lake; and he will often, if he be crooked, lie in a compound of bracken and long grass, which will adequately test his powers of recovery. There are also bunkers,

29

though these, with commendable wisdom, have been put in but sparingly at first, and, at the moment of writing, the foozler's cup of anguish is not yet filled to the brim.

As is increasingly becoming the fashion with modern courses, there are a good many one-shot holes; there are, to be precise, four, or, if we can drive a quite abnormal distance, we may include the tenth and say there are five. Of these the seventh hole over the brook before mentioned is the best : indeed it is quite one of the most charming of short holes. Its special virtue is to be found in the fact that we have to approach it at a peculiarly diabolical angle, so that the green becomes exceedingly narrow; a slice takes us into the brook, a pull into a road, and, in short, nothing but a good shot will do. Of the other short holes the most superficially terrifying, to those at least who sometimes drive a little lower than the angels, is the sixteenth, where we must stand on a little peninsula that juts out into the lake and carry some hundred or more yards of water.

Of the longer holes, all need sound and straight play, and some are thoroughly interesting. There is perhaps just a tinge of monotony about the sequence of long holes that begin after the eleventh; they are all good holes, but we might reasonably yearn for a little break in the middle. The twelfth is perhaps the best of them, since not only is it narrow, but it has the peculiar quality, granted to some holes, of a terrifying appearance. There is really plenty of room; the trees and the lake to the right are, in fact, a long way off, and ought to be omitted from our calculations,

CASSIOBURY PARK

The new eighteenth hole

but it is hard not to keep one eye on them—and off the ball. The seventeenth is another difficult hole, especially as it comes on us before we have fully recovered from the watery terrors of the sixteenth. There is a fine carry for the second over a stream that runs just in front of the green, and the brave man goes for his four, and haply takes six, while the coward plays his second with an iron and a measure of contemptible prudence, trusting thereby to secure a steady five; let us hope that he hits his pitch off the heel of his club and takes six after all.

Of all the race of park courses, it would scarcely be possible, in point of sheer beauty, to beat **Cassiobury Park,** near Watford in Hertfordshire. Neither by laying too much emphasis on its beauty do I mean to cast an oblique slur upon the golf itself, a great deal of which is very good. Of course you will not think it good if you hate trees, because there are a great many trees; and you will probably be at least once or twice hopelessly stymied by them in the course of the round. Even the most confirmed tree-hater, however, might find his heart softening, because these particular trees are so very lovely. There are the most glorious avenues, elms and limes and chestnuts and beeches, that stretch across the park, and a fine day at Cassiobury comes within measurable distance of heaven. It is even beautiful on a wet day, and the last day that I spent there was wet, quite beyond the ordinary. I remember it very well from the circumstance of having to wade breast high into drenching nettles after a ball which my wretched partner had put there. This occurred at the third hole—a hole which is rather a remarkable one in itself, and was never more remarkably played than on that occasion.

The green can be reached easily enough with one honest blow, but there is a huge tree immediately to the right of the green, and a still more huge and infinitely more alarming pit immediately under the tee. The pit is very deep and its sides precipitous, and it is altogether a very formidable affair. Our opponents drove off, I remember, and perpetrated an ordinary 'fluff' or foozle, which left the ball on grass, it is true, but at the very bottom of the pit.

"Now," said I to my partner, no doubt foolishly, "here is our chance." By way of answer he struck the ball violently on some portion of the club that lay far behind the heel. The ball dashed away at a terrific pace in the direction of square leg, came into collision with the branch of a tree some fifty yards off the line, whence it bounded back into the bed of nettles before mentioned. By some miracle the ball was dislodged from the nettles, and joined its fellow at the bottom of the pit. Then began a game the object of which an intelligent foreigner would probably have imagined to be the hitting of the ball up the bank in such a way as it should roll down exactly to the place whence it started. Ultimately, for I must pass over the intervening events, I missed a short putt to win the hole in eight.

If this third hole is the most terrifying to the habitual foozler, the more mature golfer will be a great deal more frightened of the fourth and tenth, which were really very good holes indeed. That drive at the tenth down a pretty

SANDY LODGE

The first green, looking towards the club-house

glade between the trees is, as far as appearances go at least, one of the narrowest I know, and the second shot is a good one too, though by no means so long as it used to be, with a gutty. After this tenth comes another capital 'two-shotter,' which has been made by the expedient of running two poorish holes into one, and in this case two blacks have emphatically made a white, for the second shot over another pit, only a little less disastrous than the first, is excellent.

There are several more long, slashing holes on the way back, and at one of them I recollect that our adversaries in this same adventurous foursome lost their ball within four yards of the tee, and, in spite of the most arduous and unremitting search, had to give up the hole. I must add that the drive was neither a high nor a straight one, and that the grass at the edge of the course, or as I once heard an Irish green-keeper call them, the 'sidings,' were distinctly long.

One good point about Cassiobury is the smooth and velvety surface of the green. They are a little slow and easy perhaps, but very true and soothing to putt upon, and have been wonderfully improved of late years. Time was when the very springy park turf seemed determined never to settle down into a good putting substance, but unremitting care and hard work has changed all that. Finally, I ought to add that owing to the taking in of some new land and the abandoning of some of the old holes, the course is practically in a transition stage, and so I must be pardoned if I have used the antiquated numbering of the holes.

GOLF COURSES

Of the courses to be reached from the Baker Street end of London, such as Northwood, Chorleywood, Harewood Downs and Sandy Lodge, **Northwood** is perhaps the best known, and there we come upon a somewhat different kind of golf; perhaps it would be more accurate to describe it as a mixture of two different kinds of golf. There are holes among the gorse, and there are holes of a more agricultural character among the hedges and ditches. Regarded in the abstract, gorse-bushes, or, as I ought to call them, whins, are not an ideal hazard. It is often impossible to play the ball out of them, and still more often unwise to make the attempt without a suit of armour, while the local rule, to be found on some courses, that the ball may or even must be lifted and dropped under a penalty is thoroughly unsatisfactory.

If, however, whins are from their nature a bad hazard, they have nevertheless very distinguished sanction. They are to be found on links of undoubted eminence, and were found on many more till they were literally hacked and hewed out of existence by the niblick shots of their infuriated victims. Moreover, say what we will, they are rather entertaining, and the very fact that a serious error will almost ruin us gives a poignancy which is lacking in any but the most desperate of sand-pits; we trifle pleasurably with our terrors and snatch a fearful joy. Certainly there is a great deal of amusement to be extracted from the Northwood whins, and our achievements or disasters among them are those that remain graven on the memory. Yet there is one hole in the county of ditches and hedges

NORTHWOOD

'Death or glory' (the eighth hole)

(such colossal hedges as those at Northwood were surely never seen before) that leaves as vivid an impression on the mind as the spikiest of gorse can leave elsewhere. This is the eighth, which rejoices, I believe, in the appropriate name of 'Death or Glory.' It supplies a standing refutation of the theory that a hole cannot be a good one if it is of that mongrel length known as 'a drive and a pitch,' or, as it has been brilliantly though indelicately expressed, 'a kick and a spit.'

We walk to the very brink of destruction without knowing it, for there is nothing particular to mark the drive; we have but to hit moderately straight, as it appears, over a flat and somewhat muddy space towards a bunker in the distance. Then as we walk up to the ball the full horror of our situation bursts upon us. We have to pitch over a bunker straight in front of the green, but that is mere child's play, and only the beginning of our task. On the left-hand side, eating its way into the very heart of the green, is another bunker, very deep and shored up by precipitous black timbers, and the very slightest pull on our approach shot will land us in it. The obvious thing to do would appear to be to push our approach out to the right at any cost, but that will not do either, for on a bank on the right hand side grows a perfect thicket of thorn bushes, where there is very snug lying for the ball and great scope for the niblick. It is surprising and rather humiliating to find how difficult it is to play a perfectly ordinary, straightforward mashie pitch, if only there are enough difficulties to strike terror into the soul. Were there more holes like this, the reproach implied in the term 'a drive and a pitch' would very soon disappear.

From Liverpool Street Station the municipal golfer of London takes his way either to Chingford, where he plays in a red coat under the auspices of the Corporation, or to Hainault Forest, where the County Council has recently made a playground for him. The best known, however, and probably the best of these Essex courses is **Romford**, which was for a good many years the home green of the great Braid. Indeed even now 'J. Braid (Walton Heath)' looks just a little unfamiliar to me; I still feel as if Romford ought to be the word inside the brackets. I recollect that almost the first time I played at Romford was in an open amateur competition, for which there was a very good and representative entry of London amateurs. I think it shows how much the general standard of amateur golf has gone up, that the winning score was 164 (84+80) by Mr. Mure Fergusson. Certainly Mr. Fergusson was not in his best form, but this score was good enough to win, and to win quite comfortably. There was, as far as I can remember, nothing amiss with the weather, and even making every allowance for gutty balls, it does seem extraordinary that so many people should play so supremely ill. It would be far less likely to happen to-day.

Nevertheless Romford is not a course that one would choose for the doing of a low score, for it is neither short nor easy, and is a great deal better golf than it looks. Its appearance is not particularly attractive, because in the first place it is flat, and in the second there are hedges and

ROMFORD

The sixth green

LONDON

trees to be seen. Braid himself speaks of it in Nisbet's
Golf Year Book as a "very good park course." The
adjective may well be allowed to pass, but to call it a
'park' course conveys a wrong impression, to my mind
at least; it is too open for the description to be quite appropriate, though I admit I can think of no better word.

If a course has really good putting greens and demands
that the ball should be hit consistently far and straight,
then there is a good deal to be said for it, and these virtues
must be conceded to Romford. You must hit straight or
you will be in a bunker, or 'tucked up' behind a tree; you
must hit far or you will not get up to the green in the right
number of strokes. The fourth and fifth are two as long
holes as come consecutively on any course, except Blackheath, and the fifth is an especially good one. Better than
either I like the seventh with its narrow tee-shot between
the trees and that out of bounds territory that comes
creeping in to catch you on the right. It is a hole that,
in colloquial language, 'wants a lot of playing.'

There are really quite a lot more fine holes—the tenth,
for instance, with a tremendous carrying second over a
pond, and the fourteenth, where the player is fairly hemmed
in with trees and hedges, and must drive as straight as an
arrow. When Braid was there he accomplished some
ridiculous scores in the sixties, but ordinary people will find
that anything in the seventies is quite good enough for them,
and that many a hole that ought to be done in four will, in
fact, be done in five or more. Especially is this the case
when the going is at all heavy, for Romford can on occasions

37

be just a little soft and muddy. It is probably, like a great many other inland courses, at its best in spring or autumn, for then the putting greens are really a pleasure to putt upon.

Now we come to the links of the Royal **Blackheath** Golf Club, which is very justly proud of the fact that it was instituted in 1608. That is indeed a great record, and, as we hack our ball along with a driving mashie out of a hard and flinty lie, narrowly avoiding the slaughter of a passing pedestrian, we feel that we are on hallowed ground. Moreover, though we may speak flippantly of the bad lies and the numerous live hazards on the course, the golf is good golf—far better and more searching than is to be found on many smoothly shaven lawns covered with artificial ramparts. If we desire to test our real sentiments about any particular course, it is no bad plan to imagine that we have to play a match over it against some horribly good opponent —an enemy whom, even in the moment of our most idiotic vanity, we admit to be our superior. Out of this test Blackheath comes well, for I can hardly imagine that anyone would choose to play a match with Braid, for example, over those famous seven holes if he had any other battle-ground open to him.

There are but seven holes; but of those seven, two are of a truly prodigious length, and, to make the matter worse, they are consecutive. Some idea of the length and difficulty of the course may be gleaned from the record score for the twenty-one holes, which constitute a medal round. People have been struggling round since the reign

BLACKHEATH

Signalling 'all clear'

of James I., and the record stands at 95, which, according to my arithmetic, is eleven over an average of four a hole. The record of nearly every other well-known course in the kingdom is under an average of four. To accomplish a score of under 100 at Blackheath is something to be proud of, and in the gutty days, in which I sometimes struggled round the historic course, an average of five a hole was considered, not without reason, quite good enough to win one's match against highly respectable opponents.

They let us down easily to begin with at Blackheath with quite a short first hole, only a good cleek shot being required to carry a sort of shallow pit that has very poor lying at the bottom of it; so we ought to have one three to reduce the average of the sixes and sevens that are sure to follow. The second and third are longer, but yet not hideously long, and we play them reasonably well, if we do not come into collision with public highways and the posts and rails that guard them. We may possibly have to thread our way through two teams of small boys playing football, and there are almost certain to be a nursery maid or two in the way, or an old gentleman sitting on a seat, blandly unconscious that his position is one fraught with peril to himself and annoyance to us. However, as we are forcibly clad in red coats for a danger-signal and preceded by a fore-caddie, as if we were traction engines, we may with luck and patience do fairly well.

After the third we are confronted with the two long holes, and the piling up of our score begins. It is now some time since I played them, and they are, besides, too long to describe in detail. I have a vision of reaching, after several shots on the flat, a deep hollow on the left, and spending some further time in hacking the ball along its hard and inhospitable turf, finally to emerge on to the flat again and reach the green in a score verging upon double figures. The fifth hole may be described as the same, only not quite so much so, and the round ends with two holes of a somewhat milder character, but neither of them in the least easy. Then off we go over the pit again for our second round, and there is yet another one left to play. To play three rounds over Blackheath on a cold, blustery winter's day is a man's task.

It is sad that there was no contemporary chronicler to do for the old golfers of Blackheath what John Nyren of immortal memory did for the cricketers of Hambledon; but the club has not lacked its *vates sacer*, and in Mr. W. E. Hughes' book is a store of pleasant and interesting history. Most golfers know the delightful picture of the gentleman in a red coat with blue facings, gold epaulettes and knee-breeches, who stands in so dignified an attitude, his club over his shoulder. It is dedicated to the "Society of Golfers at Blackheath" with "just respect" by their "most humble servant Lemuel Francis Abbott," and, like the artist, we too salute with just respect a venerable and illustrious society.

The Royal Wimbledon Club was founded some two hundred and sixty years after the Royal Blackheath, and yet golf is still so young a game in England that the two appear of almost equally hoary antiquity. There is an

WIMBLEDON

On the common

old-fashioned air about the golf at **Wimbledon**—an atmosphere of red coats and friendly foursomes made up at luncheon, which is exceedingly pleasant—nor is the actual golf on Wimbledon Common by any means to be despised. It has at least one supreme virtue—that of naturalness; those great clumps of gorse and the deep ravines where the birches grow were put there by the hand of Nature herself, who, if she be not so cunning, is at any rate infinitely more artistic than any golfing architect. When Mr. Horace Hutchinson wrote the Badminton volume he wrote of the golf at Wimbledon that it was almost ''an insult to the game to dignify it by the name of golf,'' adding that he would rather call it a '' wonderful substitute for the game within so short a distance of Charing Cross.'' It is perhaps a just criticism, but what would Mr. Hutchinson say of the hundred ' mud-heaps ' that have sprung up within a short distance of Charing Cross since these days? He would probably keep silence lest he should fall a victim to the law of libel and an unsympathetic jury.

Certainly the lies at Wimbledon are not good; they are hard and flinty, and at certain places, in particular the long second hole, they have seemed to me at times almost the worst in the world. But there is this measure of compensation in hard turf, that it always bears some resemblance, however dim and remote, to the ' real thing '; it is infinitely more inspiriting than the soft and spongy lawns, which may be truer and smoother, but are removed by a far wider gulf from the golf that *is* golf.

If the Royal Wimbledon golfer dislikes a crowd or a red

coat, or if, being a very wicked man or a very busy one, he wishes to play on Sunday, he need nowadays only walk out of the back door of his club-house instead of his front door, and he is on his own private course at Cæsar's Camp. A wonderful place is this new Wimbledon course, for as soon as we are on it all signs of men, houses and omnibuses, and the other symptoms of a busy suburb disappear as if by magic, and a prospect of glorious solitary woods stretches away into the distance in every direction. Only at one place, where the new course verges on the Common, do we see such a thing as a house, and our friend Charing Cross might be a hundred miles away. Like the egg, the course is good in parts: very good as long as we are among the whins on the hard ground which is the ground of the Common: rather soft and muddy when we are on the meadows lower down. Taking the two courses together, the men of Wimbledon have much to be thankful for.

There is still one London course that assuredly deserves mention, that of Prince's Golf Club on **Mitcham Common**. Roads and lamp-posts and, ugliest of all, tramways have not added to its loveliness. But it is still a delightful place, with a good deal of solitary beauty left. There is abundance of gorse here too, but the impression produced is quite different from that at Wimbledon. The ground is flatter, and one can take in a greater stretch at one glance; it is not broken up, as it were, into districts by gullies and ravines, and one misses the pretty birch trees of Wimbledon.

Courses that are not protected by a ring-fence of privacy

42

MITCHAM

The seventh green

are not as a rule notable for the goodness of their greens, since every now and then a cantankerous commoner is apt to drive a waggon across them by way of asserting his rights. At Prince's, however, they have really beautiful greens, big and rolling and grassy, which are a joy to putt upon, and there is a further distinction between Mitcham and other common courses, that the making of artificial bunkers has been allowed to supplement Nature in an unobtrusive measure.

There are plenty of good two-shot holes where, if we do not quite need the brassey for our second shot, we must yet give the ball a downright, honest hit with some iron club that is not too much lofted.

The first, seventh, fifteenth, and seventeenth—to mention only four—are all good holes, the drive at the fifteenth being rendered the more alarming by a pond which traps a hooked ball. The twelfth hole also has a rather frightening tee-shot over the corner of a garden—a sort of Stationmaster's Garden in miniature—with the possibility of slicing into what was once a manufactory of explosives.

Mitcham is essentially a course for the leisured golfer. It is comparatively useless to the busy man, since he may not play there on Sunday, and to do so on Saturday is a vexation of spirit. Granted, however, a reasonably dry day in mid-week, and there is certainly no pleasanter golf to be found within so short and easy a journey from London.

CHAPTER III.

KENT AND SUSSEX.

THERE is always something stirring in a roll of illustrious names, and for the mere sensual pleasure of writing them I set them down in order at the beginning of the chapter—Sandwich, Deal, Prince's, Littlestone, and Rye, in the counties of Kent and Sussex. Each of the five has devoted adherents who will maintain its merits against the world in heated argument, but there can be little doubt which has the right to come first. It would be showing a sad disrespect to golfing history, very recent history though it be, to begin otherwise than with the links of the Royal St. George's Golf Club at Sandwich.

For a course that is still comparatively young—the club was instituted in 1887—**Sandwich** has had more than its share of ups and downs. It was heralded with much blowing of trumpets and without undergoing any period of probation, burst full-fledged into fame. For some time it would have ranked only a degree below blasphemy to have hinted at any imperfection. Then came a time when impious wretches, who had the temerity to think for them-

44

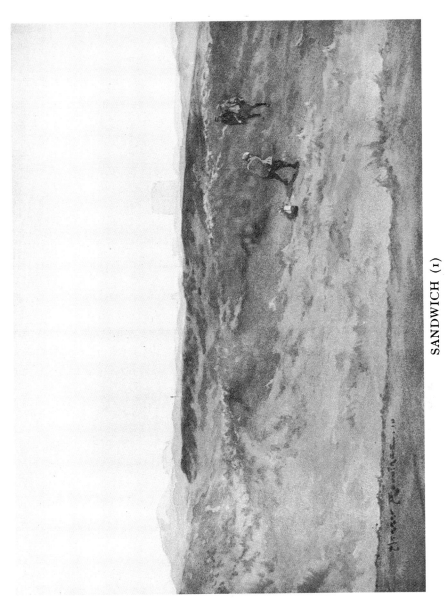

SANDWICH (1)

The 'Sahara'

selves, began to whisper that there were faults at Sandwich, that it was nothing but a driver's course, that the whole art of golf did not consist of hitting a ball over a sandhill and then running up to the top to see what had happened on the other side. Gradually the multitude caught up the cry of the few, till nobody, who wished to put forward a claim to a critical faculty, had a good word to say for the course. Then the club began to set its house in order, lengthening here and bunkering there, not without a somewhat bitter controversy between the moderates and the progressives, until the pendulum has begun to swing back, and poor Sandwich is coming to its own again.

Throughout all this controversial warfare one fact has remained unchanged, namely, that, whatever they may think of its precise merits as a test of golf, most golfers unite in liking to play there. The humbler player frankly enjoys hitting over his sandhill largely because of the frequency with which he hits into it: the superior person may despise the sandhill and may be utterly bored with it anywhere else, but he retains a sneaking affection for it at Sandwich. It attracts him in spite of himself and his, as some people think them, tedious views.

Sandwich has a charm that belongs to itself, and I frankly own myself under the spell. The long strip of turf on the way to the seventh hole, that stretches between the sandhills and the sea; a fine spring day, with the larks singing as they seem to sing nowhere else; the sun shining on the waters of Pegwell Bay and lighting up the white cliffs in the distance; this is as nearly my idea of Heaven as is

45

to be attained on any earthly links. "Confound their politics," one feels disposed to cry, "frustrate their knavish tricks! Why do they want to alter this adorable place? I know they are perfectly right, and I have even agreed with them that this is a blind shot and that an indefensibly bad hole, but what does it all matter? This is perfect bliss." Of course Sandwich is capable of improvement, and will doubtless be improved; whatever happens, the larks will continue to twitter, the sun will still be shining on Pegwell Bay : the charm can never be gone. It is at any rate very delightful now, and so let us go and play the first hole and enjoy ourselves without being too desperately critical.

One great characteristic—I think it is a beauty—of Sandwich is the extraordinary solitude that surrounds the individual player. We wind about in the dells and hollows among the great hills, alone in the midst of a multitude, and hardly ever realize that there are others playing on the links until we meet them at luncheon. Thus, on the first tee, we may catch a glimpse of somebody playing the last hole, and another couple disappearing over the brow to the second, and that is all; the rest is sandhills and solitude.

And now we must positively cease from our reflections and get off that first tee, with a fine raking shot that shall carry us over the insidious and fatal little hollow called the 'kitchen.' If we are clear of it, another good shot will take us home over a deep cross-bunker on to the green, big, smooth, and beautiful, as are all the greens at Sandwich.

46

SANDWICH (2)

Playing on to the green from 'Hades'

KENT AND SUSSEX

At the second we have a bunker to carry from the tee—
it was sometimes a terrible carry for a gutty—and then
a pitch on to a plateau green, the sides whereof slope down
steeply into hollows on either side. This shot was once
a great bone of contention, and in truth success was
formerly somewhat a matter of luck, for the ball pitched
on a hog's back and kicked sometimes straight on to the
hole and sometimes to the right or left. Now, however,
the hog's back has been smoothed and flattened, and if
we play the proper shot we shall get a four to hearten us
up for the drive over the Sahara.

When a name clings to a hole we may be sure that there
is something in that hole to stir the pulse, and in fact there
are few more absolute joys than a perfectly hit shot that
carries the heaving waste of sand which confronts us on
the third tee. The shot is a blind one, and we have not
the supreme felicity of seeing the ball pitch and run down
into the valley to nestle by the flag. We see it for a long
time, however, soaring and swooping over the desert, and,
when it finally disappears, we have a shrewd notion as to
its fate. If the wind be fresh against us, we must play
away to the right for safety, and the glorious enjoyment
of the hole is gone, but even so a good shot will be repaid,
and every yard that we can go to the left may make the
difference between a difficult and an easy second.

On the very next tee another bunker of terrible aspect
lies before us, this time a towering mountain of sand, and
the ball is soon out of sight. However, at the second shot
we get a good view of the green, away in the distance

47

perched up on a plateau hard up against a fence. There is rough to the right and a bunker almost in the line to the left, but a good shot will carry it, and, after the ball has vanished for a moment, it will reappear, trickling gently along the plateau to the hole side; it is really a grand two-shot hole.

At the fifth the sandhills begin to close in upon us, but a fair straight drive should land the ball safely in the valley; this hole is now in the melting pot, and is being transformed from a three into a four. We will, therefore, avoid a painful controversy and tee our ball before the famous 'Maiden.' Few bunkers have a more infamous reputation than this Maiden, but the new-comer to the Sandwich of to-day will think that she has done little to deserve it. There stands the Maiden, steep, sandy, and terrible, with her face scarred and seamed with black timbers, but alas! we have no longer to drive over her crown: we hardly do more than skirt the fringe of her garment. In old days the tee was right beneath the highest pinnacle, and sheer terror made the shot formidable, but the tee-shots to the fifth endangered the lives of those driving to the sixth, and the tee had to be put far away to the right. The present Maiden is but a shadow of its old self, and the splendour of it has in a great measure departed.

My pen has run away with me over the first six holes, as I knew it would, and there still remain twelve more holes to play. 'Hades' will, no doubt, deserve its name if we top our tee-shot, though otherwise it is a reasonably easy three, but the ninth is in reality a far more formidable affair. The hole will doubtless be called the 'Corsets' for ever, but the second of these two famous bunkers now plays but an inconsiderable part, for the reformers have moved the green far on and away to the left and, it must be admitted, have made a good hole out of a very bad one.

We may still drive into the first Corset, however, and if we do, Heaven help us! We shall be playing a nightmare game of racquets against its unflinching sides, and the other man will win the hole.

With the turn at Sandwich the nature of the course begins to alter, and in place of doing threes—or perchance sevens—among the hills, we shall be travelling over the flatter ground in a series of steady fives, with, let us hope, an occasional four. There are plenty of good holes— better, perhaps, than some on the way out—but they do not make the same appeal to the imagination, nor are they so characteristic. One, at least, deserves a special word of mention, the fourteenth, or 'Suez Canal,' where many and many a second shot has found a watery grave. Those who love the hopes and fears of a lucky-bag will enjoy the seventeenth, where the hole lies in a deep dell with sharply sloping sides. Man can direct the ball into the dell, but only Providence can decide its subsequent fate, and whether it will lie stone dead or a round dozen of yards away is a matter of chance. There is no chance about the last hole, where we must hit two good, long, straight shots; it is a fine finish, and will leave us with happy recollections as we take our way to one or other of the neighbouring courses. We are in the midst of a perfect tangle of courses,

D   49

since within easy reach are Deal, Prince's, Kingsdown, and St. Augustine's, at Ebbsfleet.

The **Deal** course is little more than a stone's throw away from Sandwich. It is the same kind of country, the same, or very nearly the same, kind of turf, and yet the general impression produced by it is quite different.

There is this difference to begin with, that it is less remote and solitary. The club-house stands on a high road and the outskirts of the town come creeping out to the edge of the links. Men, women and children, butchers' and bakers' carts pass and re-pass along the road : there are live creatures to be seen engaged in other avocations than golfing, and, altogether, as compared with Sandwich, the scene is one of business and bustle. The links themselves are more open : one might almost say more bleak of aspect; there are not so many little secret hollows and valleys between the hills; Deal is altogether less snug (I can think of no better word) than Sandwich.

To say this is to make no comparison of the merits of the two courses, which is an unnecessary and invidious thing to do. It is quite enough to say that the golf at Deal is very good indeed—fine, straight-ahead, long-hitting golf, wherein the fives are likely to be many and the fours few. There are those that contend that it is almost superhumanly difficult, but unless there be a high wind, I think that they exaggerate a little. The difficulty lies in hitting far enough, and not so much in the intrinsic terrors of the holes. If we can hit far enough to carry the hummocky country and attain the region of good lies : if, in short, we are long

DEAL

Playing the 'Sandy Parlour'

drivers, we need fear no particularly subtle devilry, but the driving has to be something more than merely decent.

It seems a topsy-turvy procedure, but a description of the Deal course ought to begin with the last four holes, for they are its particular joy and pride, and have attained a fame equal to that of the last four holes—the 'loop'— at Prestwick. Certainly they make a spirited and exciting finish to a round, for they need good play and—this with bated breath—good luck. The difficulty of the fifteenth lies in the second shot, which must be played with a measure of accuracy and fortune on to the crest of a ridge, from which it will totter slowly down a sloping green to the hole. Play the shot the least bit too gingerly and the ball will refuse to climb the ridge; too hard and it will inevitably race across the green into rough grass, while the chances of recovering from a faulty second with a little pitching shot from off the green are not great. Certainly it is a difficult hole, and so is the next; indeed, with the wind in the right quarter, this sixteenth hole is one of the finest imaginable. We see the flag away there in the far distance, waving upon a small plateau. Immediately below the plateau to the left lies a little valley of inglorious security, but away to the right and beyond the green are ruts and long grass, and the second shot has to be as accurate as it is long. That is supposing that we can get there in two at all, but alas! that is often impossible, and therein, to my thinking, lies a certain weakness of the hole. A particularly elastic tee or series of tees seems to be needed so that the hole can be made a two-shot hole, even when the wind is adverse. At present the longest driver must often be content to reach the green with a pitch for his third, and is denied the crowning triumph of a critical second shot successfully accomplished. A wind against us at the sixteenth diminishes sensibly the sum total of enjoyment of the round, for that second shot is such an inspiring one. The green stands there waiting to be won, defying us to reach it, and to abandon the attempt without a struggle is sad work.

Of the seventeenth I feel bound to say, with all just respect, that it appears to be one of the very luckiest holes—in the matter of approaching—that ever was made, but the eighteenth is a noble hole, with that little narrow plateau green that will yield to no mere rule of thumb approaching. If we pitch the ball on the face of the slope, nothing will induce it to go further, while if we pitch on the green we are almost inevitably too far. He reaps a rich reward who can play a low, skimming shot which shall pitch on the flat and then run on full of life and clamber up the hill. It is *the* hole *par excellence* for the man who learned to approach at St. Andrews.

There are many holes at Deal which are in every respect as good as the last four, if indeed they are not better. What could be finer than the second, where we travel almost from tee to green along a ridge that kicks away to right or left anything but the perfect shot—what, too, of the sixth, where, with a great shot and a big wind at our backs, we may hope for a three, but where far more often we must play the cunningest of pitches on to the most slippery of table-lands in order to get a four? What a jolly view there is from that green with the sea close beneath us and perhaps a glimpse of a big liner in the distance!

The fourth hole, 'The Sandy Parlour,' had for some years a great name, but, like some other blind short holes, has come gradually to live on its reputation. The shot is a blind one over a big sandy bluff, and we shall now have a far more difficult shot at the reformed fourteenth, wherein we can see from the tee exactly where we have to go in order to avoid a very great deal of trouble. When all is said, however, the short holes at Deal are not its strong point, and it is those long, raking holes which we ought to have done in fours that leave the pleasantest memories.

Close to the links of Sandwich, so close that in trying to carry the Suez Canal we may slice to within its precincts, lies another very fine golf course, **Prince's** to wit, the newest among the select band of really first-class seaside courses. Here is a course upon which as much care and thought and affection have been spent as on any in the world, and they have certainly not been spent in vain. It was laid out with the very highest of ideals; it was to be the good player's course, and was to trap and test and worry that self-satisfied person till he became doubtful whether he was a good player at all. A first glance at the course shows that strict attention to business is meant. Here are no fascinating mountains, no spacious water-jumps: but there is fine golfing country, broken and undulating, with smooth strips of fairway showing here and there amid the rough grass and the myriad pot-bunkers.

GOLF COURSES

Those who laid out the course at Prince's kept one aim very steadily in view, that of compelling the player to place his tee-shot. "It is not enough," they said in effect, "for him to keep out of the rough; not only must he be on the course, but he must place his ball sometimes to the right-hand side of the course, sometimes to the left. He must, if he desire to play the holes as well as they can be played, often greatly dare, but his great daring shall have its due reward." Now the best plan, in order to give a practical shape to this high ideal, is to make the hole, to use a familiar expression, 'dog-legged,' that is to say, the player does not drive his first ball straight at the hole, but has to turn at an angle to play his second shot. A hole so devised can give a great advantage to the long and daring driver who is likewise straight. The bunkering can be so arranged that he who takes great risks and hugs the rough more closely shall have an easy and an open approach, while the man who either from over-caution or insufficient accuracy has merely gone straight down the middle of the course is confronted by a more difficult second shot over a formidable array of bunkers. For this reason we find at Prince's the apotheosis of the 'dog-legged' or 'round-the-corner' holes, and some, nay nearly all of them, are about as good as they can be.

There is something of the dog-leg about the very first hole, where we drive at an angle over a ridge covered with bents. The third needs two fine shots, and the pot-bunkers rage furiously together in innumerable quantities. Then at the sixth we have one of the most charming two-shot holes to

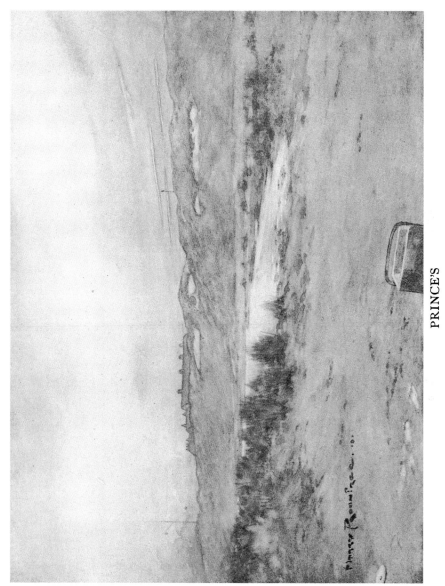

PRINCE'S

The drive from the eleventh tee

be seen anywhere, with just a suspicion of a bend in the
narrow strip of fairway, a wilderness of sandhills on the
right, and rough to the left. At the eighth we need not
place the shot with quite such dreadful accuracy, but
instead we must hit prodigiously hard and far, for after
we have hit the tee-shot a steep hill rears its sandy face
between us and the hole, and a really fine carrying brassey
shot is needed if we are to be on the green. It is more
like a Sandwich hole than a Prince's hole, and might perhaps feel more at home on the other side of the boundary
fence, but after all variety is a pleasant thing, and this
eighth brings back memories of the mighty Alps at
Prestwick, and has a splendour and a dash about it which
makes an instantaneous appeal. The eleventh is another
good hole, where, if we push our drive far enough out to
the right over the big hills, we may hope to put our second
on the green, where it nestles amid a guard of hummocks.
Nor must we omit some mention of the short holes, all
excellent in their different ways and all fiercely guarded,
where a shot has got to be something more than decently
straight, since—and this applies to the approaching in
general—the ball does not run to the hole unless it is hit
there, and the ground falls away towards the edges of the
greens.

Now after this very exacting golf we may turn to something rather easier and more straightforward and take our
tickets for New Romney in order to play at Littlestone.

New Romney is a pleasant, quiet, sleepy spot with a
fine old church, once a thriving seaport, now left high and

dry a mile or more inland. **Littlestone** consists of a long
and somewhat unprepossessing terrace of grey lodging-
houses, arranged with mathematical precision along one
side of a straight, flat road.   On the other side of the road
is the sea, and this is the saving clause at Littlestone.   It
is not beautiful—very far from it—but we are right on
the edge of the sea; we snuff it fresh and salt in our nostrils,
and can almost believe that one wave, just a little larger
than the others, could overwhelm the road and the terrace
and the very links themselves.

Yet, though we are so near the sea, and there is as
much sea and sand as anyone could wish, the course itself
has just the suspicion of an inland look.   The fairway is
so beautifully flat and shaven and runs so straight and so
precisely between two lines of thick tufty grass, which
might at certain seasons be irreverently called hay.   The
soil itself at the first two and last two holes is not altogether
above the accusation of being clay; it can be rather muddy
in winter and terribly hard in summer.   No; I cannot get
it out of my head that Littlestone does look like one of
the trimmest and smoothest of inland courses picked up
by some benevolent magician and dumped down again by
the sea.

However, we have all been taught that we ought not to
judge by appearances, and that people cannot help their
looks.   Bearing this in mind, we shall find that the appearance of Littlestone does not do it justice, and that there
is in fact very good golf to be played there.   Moreover,
it is much better golf than it used to be, since with Braid,

LITTLESTONE

The carry from the seventeenth tee

as the villain-in-chief, and Mr. F. W. Maude, as second conspirator, a vast number of pot-bunkers have been scattered about the course, and Littlestone is no longer the paradise it once was for the erratic slogger. If the course has a weakness now it is no longer a lack of bunkers; rather is it something, that no human ingenuity can alter, a uniform flatness of stances and lies. Shot after shot has to be played from a perfectly smooth, flat plain; there are none of the little hills and hummocks that add so much to the fascination and the difficulty of Deal and Rye.

Still if there are no little hills, there are, at any rate, some alarmingly big ones, and the holes that we remember best are those that are mountainous and more than a little blind. At the second, after driving down a shaven avenue, we have an imposing second shot to play over a big hill, which is made the more terrifying by two bunkers in its face. The sixteenth is another fine slashing hole, where we have to make a momentous decision, whether to try heroically for a four or ingloriously for a five. In old days it was really a case of Hobson's choice. It was hopeless to attempt to carry over that cavernous bunker cut in the face of the hill, and there was nothing for it but to play a dull, safe second, and hop over with the third shot. Now, however, a short cut, a kind of north-west passage, has been cut through the rough ground to the left, and two shots, perfectly steered and perfectly struck, will see the ball disappear over the hill-top to lie in safety on the big, flat green beyond.

These two are of the more flamboyant order of hole,

but there are others less imposing, but quite as good. At the eleventh there is one of those uncomfortable tee-shots, which are so excellent. There is a canal, a nasty, insidious serpentine beast of a canal, which winds its way along the left-hand side of the course, and it is our duty, in order to gain distance, to hug it as close as we dare; yet if we show ourselves the least bit too affectionate towards it, this ungrateful canal will assuredly engulf our ball to our utter destruction. To push the ball too far out to the right is to make our second shot unpleasantly long, and it is a hard shot, one that we desire to make as short as possible. Bunkers guard the corners of the green, and the putting is billowy and difficult; in fact, a four is far more likely to win the hole than to halve it. There are plenty more good holes: the ninth, a short hole, which demands the most accurate of iron shots, and the fourth, with its green on a sloping, narrow neck among the hills. The lies at Littlestone are flat and easy, but they will not be a bit too easy for some of the shots we shall have to play from them.

"Kent, sir—everybody knows Kent—apples, cherries, hops and women," observed Mr. Jingle, and to-day he might properly add "and golf courses"; but now we must leave Kent and cross the Sussex border to get to **Rye**— and there are surely few pleasanter places to get to. It looks singularly charming as the train comes sliding in on a long curve, with the sullen flat marshes on the left and the tall cliff on the right, while straight in front are the red roofs of the town huddled round the old church. We have only a few yards to walk along a narrow little street;

RYE

The fifteenth green

then we twist round to the right up a steep little hill and under the Land Gate and we are at the Dormy House, old and red and overgrown with creepers. Rye is such a friendly, quiet spot; never in a hurry, and never with the least appearance of being full, save, perhaps, for a short time in the summer, when it is infested with artists. It is the ideal place for the golfer who is wearied out with a fortnight's fruitless balloting at St. Andrews, which has resulted in his once drawing a time, and that at 12.30.

At Rye we just loaf down, without the least anxiety, to the little steam tram which is to carry us—with a prodigious deal of panting and snorting—out to the links at Camber. This, indeed, is the one disadvantage of Rye, that the golf is not at our front door-step. Rye still stands upon a cliff, but it is a cliff that the waters have long ceased to trouble, and Camber, where the links are, is two miles away. However, when we do get there, the golf is as good, or very nearly as good, as is to be found anywhere.

The two great features of golf at Rye are the uniformly fiendish behaviour of the wind and the fascinating variety of the stances. The wind presumably blows no harder than it does anywhere else, but the holes are so contrived that the prevailing wind, which comes off the sea, is always blowing across us. With a typical Rye wind blowing, it may be said that there is but one hole where it blows straight in our teeth, and one—and that a short one— where it is straight behind us. At the other sixteen holes the enemy persists in making a flanking attack upon us, and we never have a perfectly straightforward shot to play,

GOLF COURSES

For the few who are artists in using the wind, Rye is a paradise; for the majority who are not, it is a place of trial and disillusionment.

Disillusioned too will be they who imagine that they know all that there is to be known about wooden clubs, because they have attained to some certainty in hitting a ball that lies teed on a smooth, level plain. At Rye they must be prepared to hit brassey shots—and long, straight brassey shots, too—with one foot on a hummock and the other in a pit. If they cannot do it, they must be content to take five far more often than they like.

For these two reasons it is a fine course on which to give strokes, and an ideal battle-ground for golfing giants, from a spectator's point of view, since it is scarcely possible, even with the most perfect golf, to avoid two or three shots in the course of a round which shall be difficult enough and unusual enough to be intensely interesting.

The subtlety of the short holes is the thing that will probably impress the advanced student, while the more elementary will retain vivid recollections of the knotted horrors of the Sea hole and the utter hopelessness of the eighteenth bunker. Certainly that eighteenth bunker— we never ought to get in it—is a pit of desolation; its sides are so steep and so smooth that wherever the ball may pitch down it will roll to the bottom, ultimately to repose in a footmark. To the man who has a good medal score in prospect, it looms vast and uncarryable—a thing against which it is useless to struggle. So appalling is it that at one time some tender-hearted people thought that it was refined cruelty to keep such a horror till the last; so they shuffled the course round and turned the eighteenth hole into the ninth, in order that, if a man was fated to ruin his score, he should be put more quickly out of his agony. This was rightly considered, however, to be mistaken kindness, and the big bunker is still kept as a crowning joy or misery. The three short holes are certainly things of beauty and of the three the best and the most paralyzing is the eighth.

To see Mr. de Montmorency play this hole against a wind with a hateful little club which he calls his 'push-cleek' is to see iron play at its highest; to attempt to play it ourselves is to realize how far we fall short of that standard and to what a state of impotency and terror it is possible to be reduced by the surrounding scenery. The appearance of the hole is so frightening that the ball is as good as missed before we address it. The distance on a still day can be compassed with a nice, firm shot with the iron, but the green looks so small and the sides of the plateau on which it stands so steep and unpleasant; the angle at which we approach it is so awkward and the wind blows so persistently on our backs that something is almost sure to go, and does go, wrong.

The fourteenth is another good and difficult short hole, built in pious imitation of the eleventh at St. Andrews, as is also the fourth hole at Worplesdon, and the imitation is carried so far that it is not uncommon, after the tee-shots have been struck, to hear the agonized cry go up to Heaven, "I'm in the Eden!" This is, unfortunately, the one hole where the wind does not do its best for Rye, since it blows for days together straight behind the player and makes the stopping of the ball upon the green too much a matter of luck.

There are so many other good holes that it seems invidious to distinguish between them. There is the first, with its narrow, curly tee-shot between a stream and a road and its little square box of a green protected on every side; there are the fifth and sixth, good holes both, and one cannot leave out the third, commonly called the 'Dog-leg.' Then, coming home, what could be better than the eleventh, with its uncompromisingly small green, guarded night and day by a deep bunker and most magnetic cabbage-garden; or the sixteenth, with its long hog-back? Surely there can nowhere be anything appreciably better than the golf to be had at this truly divine spot.

Leaving Rye we may glance at two other Sussex courses of quite a different kind—Eastbourne and Ashdown Forest. **Eastbourne** is, like Brighton and Seaford, to name two other Sussex courses, a seaside course only in name. It is one of the fairly numerous clan of down courses, of which the main features, as a rule, consist of chalk, thistles, steep hills, and perplexing putting greens. It may be because I played on it at an early and impressionable age, but I think that the old nine-hole course was better golf than the present full-sized round. The best holes now to be found at Eastbourne were all among the original nine, and the newer holes exaggerate the vices of the old ones, while lacking some of their virtues. There was an old

EASTBOURNE

'Paradise'

KENT AND SUSSEX

Eastbourne golfing saying which Mr. Hutchinson has quoted, that "the ball will always come back from Beachy Head," which, being interpreted, means that there are certain slopes at Eastbourne so long and steep that it is impossible to play the ball too much to the left or right, as the case may be. No matter how crooked the shot, down will come the ball, trickling, trickling, till it lies close to the hole. Now that is not a very skilful or amusing or in any way good sort of golf, and there is a good deal of it in some of the newer holes. The old ones are not perhaps wholly free from the taint, and the putting is infinitely deceitful, but still there is less of the deplorable use of the side-wall.

Perhaps the two chief features of the course are Paradise and the Chalk Pit, and with an unfortunate prodigality nature has so disposed of them, that we have to encounter them at one and the same hole. Paradise is a pretty wood, traversed by a public road and adorned by one of those sham Greek temples which were beloved of our ancestors. The chalk pit explains itself, and it is only necessary to add that it is an extremely deep one. We drive over the pit, and a good drive will go bounding down a hill a prodigious distance, leaving us with an iron shot to play over Paradise wood on to a horse-shoe shaped green in the neighbourhood of the temple. How it may be with rubber-cored balls I do not know; probably everyone pitches jauntily and easily enough over Paradise, but it was something of a feat to carry the wood in the consulship of Plancus, and many a reasonably stout-hearted golfer would sneak round the corner and, giving the timber a wide berth, make reasonably sure of his five. One of the very finest shots I ever saw was played at this hole by Mr. Hutchinson with a horrid, hard little ball called the 'Maponite,' long since consigned to a deserved oblivion. His ball lay upon the road, whence he hit it with a full shot against the wind right over the wood on to the green.

The other hole at Eastbourne which leaves a vivid impression on the mind is the seventeenth—a long hole that is skirted closely on the right throughout its whole length by the grounds of Compton Place, a house that belongs to the Duke of Devonshire. The tee-shot gives a great opportunity for the ambitious driver who can carry just as many trees as he has a mind for, and thus make the hole a good deal shorter and easier; but the second is never a very easy one, with a spinney on the left and a sunk fence on the right guarding closely the side of the green.

To putt at Eastbourne is an art of itself. It is not that the greens are not good, for they are often excellent, but the hidden slopes in them are like Mr. Weller's knowledge of London, "extensive and peculiar." For the stranger, the safest rule is that he should take a great deal of trouble in determining where to aim, and then aim somewhere else. To add to the piquancy of the situation, the course is visited by a persistent and violent wind, rendering the golf eminently healthy, but almost exasperatingly difficult.

The **Ashdown Forest** course lies in that most delightful but alas! most rapidly built-over country near Forest Row and East Grinstead, and not very far from Crowborough,

FOREST ROW

The fifteenth green

where is another very charming course. Like Eastbourne, it can boast of some very curly and puzzling putting greens, but there the resemblance ceases. It lies not upon the downs, but upon the forest, which means among the heather, and alone of all the heathery clan, indeed almost alone among golf courses, it is as nearly as may be perfectly natural. The greens, I take it, are, some of them, in a measure artificial, but there is no such thing as an artificial hazard to be seen. Nature has been kind in supplying a variety of pits and streams to carry, and so we certainly do not notice any lack of trouble or incident. It is only at the end of the round that we realize with a pleasurable shock that there is not a single hideous rampart on the course, or so much even as a pot-bunker.

Nature is really a wonderfully good architect, when she is in a painstaking mood, and she has made few better two-shot holes than the second at Ashdown. First comes a sufficiently frightening tee-shot over a big pit, and then a really long second on to a small green, guarded in front by a stream and on either side by small grips or ditches, beyond which again is the heather. The short and humble player, or the long driver who has perforce to be humbler because of a misplaced tee-shot, can play short in two, and so home in three, but that is but poor fun; we must go for that second if we are to extract a full measure of joy from the round.

A fine slashing hole again is the sixteenth, where the green is guarded by a grass ground ditch and a low wall of earth, which one would take to be an artificial bunker that has fallen into disuse, except that it dispels the illusion by looking infinitely less ugly and more artistic. When the wind is not too strongly against us, here is a grand chance of hitting out with the brassey and reaping a due reward. Then again, for sheer terrifying splendour of appearance, what could be better than the tee-shots at the thirteenth, commonly called 'Apollyon,' and the home hole? In both cases we drive from one hillside to another, and in both cases there flows at the bottom of the valley a stream that shall engulf the feebly struck ball, to say nothing of heather and bracken and other things.

Probably, however, the best-known hole at Ashdown is the 'Island' hole, although it must be admitted that the recent alteration—and vast improvement—of the fifth hole has robbed the Island of some of its terrors. The green, which is divided into two terraces, is surrounded on all sides by streams that have clayey and precipitous banks. It can be reached from the tee with a pitch of a very modest character, and, as the hole is played now, so long as the ball is hit reasonably straight there is no such pressing need for nicety of judgment in strength. It was a different matter from the old tee, when the angle from which one played was such that the green was fairly broad but alarmingly short. A measure of crookedness went unpunished, and a certain pusillanimous shortness was not always fatal, but many a fine bold straight shot overpitched by the merest fraction of a yard found a watery grave. Moreover, it was fatally easy to lift under a penalty from one ditch only to plump into another, and so on for ever and ever. This hole has the further unique distinction of being the only endowed hole in the United Kingdom. Some time ago a member of the club settled a sum of £5 upon this hole, and the accumulated interest is to go to anyone who shall do the hole in one at the Easter, Whitsuntide, or Autumn meetings. So far the feat has been too much for the skill of the members, and the bait has apparently not grown great enough to tempt them from the paths of truth, for the interest on the £5 is still without a claimant.

No account of Ashdown would be complete without some mention of the great golfing family of Mitchell. It is very curious how artisan golf will make great strides upon one course and be non-existent at another, with no apparent reason to account for the difference. There seems no particular reason why it should flourish so greatly at Ashdown Forest, and yet the Cantelupe Club, which is the local workmans' club, can put an extraordinarily strong team in the field, and in their annual match with them regularly give the Ashdown Forest Club to the dogs and vultures. Of this team some seven or eight are usually Mitchells. One or two of them have become professionals, but the amateur members of the family, who stay at home and work at their ordinary avocations, are also redoubtable players, and successfully to beard the Mitchells in their own den, on the tricky, sloping Ashdown greens, would want a very good side indeed.

CHAPTER IV.

THE WEST AND SOUTH-WEST.

IT would clearly be unbecoming to treat the western and south-western courses in strict geographical order, because there is one honoured name which must come first, that of **Westward Ho!**—the oldest seaside golf course in England. The Royal North Devon Club was founded in 1864, and when the golf at Westward Ho! was in its infancy it was fostered and encouraged by Mr. George Glennie of St. Andrews celebrity, who played much of his golf at Blackheath, so that the famous flinty old course on the heath may claim to be a kind of god-parent to the sandhills and rushes of Northam Burrows.

To go to Westward Ho! is not to make a mere visit of pleasure as to an ordinary course; it is, as is the case of a few other great links, a reverent pilgrimage. Was it not here that Mr. Horace Hutchinson and J. H. Taylor, besides a host of other fine players, learned the game? and surely, it may be added in parenthesis, no golfing nursery has ever turned out two infant prodigies with such unique and dissimilar styles. Has it not the tallest and spikiest

68

rushes in the world, and the biggest bunker to carry from
the tee? and, lastly, has is not lately been remodelled and
reformed and made so difficult that many will compare it,
not even with bated breath, to St. Andrews.   Therefore,
the stranger, as he jogs along in the little train from
Bideford and looks out at the white horses in Barnstaple
Bay, may be pardoned if he is in a state of suppressed
excitement and full of the highest hopes.   In truth, it is
a splendid course for which he is bound, and not only is
it wonderfully difficult and wonderfully interesting, but it
has a charm that is given to but few links.   It looks more
like a good golf course than almost any other course in
the world.   Not perhaps when we first emerge from the
club-house, for the first three holes lie upon a rather flat
and marshy piece of ground, but as soon as we get to the
fourth hole it is obvious that the burrows were ordained
by providence for no other than their present purpose.
From the high tee to the fifth hole we get a view of a perfect
stretch of golfing country, broken and undulating with the
sandhills on the left and a vast expanse of rushes on the
right, for, in spite of much pruning and uprooting, there
are still plenty of the famous rushes left.   It is a sight to
make glad the heart of man, and at the same time to fill
him with gloomy doubts as to whether he is quite good
enough to play upon such a course.

Another great attraction about Westward Ho! is its
supreme naturalness.   It looks for all the world as if some
golfing adventurer had merely had to stroll out with a hole-
cutter, a bundle of flags, and perhaps a light roller, and had

made the course in less than no time. Many bunkers have been cut, of course, but with one exception they look quite inartificial, and do not take away from the wonderful impression of naturalness made by the greens. Sometimes the hole is on a plateau or in a hollow, and then it is obvious that Nature and not any human architect has been at work; no man could have devised those jutting promontories, those little irregular bays, which are so alluring. Sometimes, again, the greens lie flat and open, and then they blend so imperceptibly and harmoniously with the surrounding country that it is impossible to say where the green ends and " through the green " begins, for the turf is quite beautiful. Some years ago a pestilence of weeds seized upon it, and the lies and greens of Westward Ho! were in grave danger of losing their reputation, but with infinite patience and trouble the weeds have been removed and the turf is once more itself again, crisp and smooth, and withal full of life and run.

It has often been said and written that the feature of the golf at Westward Ho! is that the ball must be placed with each shot, and it is, I think, on the whole, a sound criticism. It is often possible to hit the ball very crooked without being immediately punished, but in nearly every case the next shot will be an exceedingly difficult one. I do not know the course quite as well as I could wish, but the seventh hole comes into my head as a good example. Here it is possible to pull considerably from the tee without getting anything but a perfect lie, but then, between the player and the hole, close to the green, there stretches a

WESTWARD HO!

The carry at the fifth tee

phalanx of pot-bunkers, whereas the man who has played well out to the right over the guiding flag, has an easy and open approach.   At the ninth, again, there is vast prairie into which to drive, but it is only by keeping well out to the right that we shall be able to hook the ball round on to that cunning plateau green; that little pot-bunker in the face of the plateau will most effectually put the man who has hooked from the tee, into a quandary.

It is not perhaps quite justifiable to include wind in a list of the permanent difficulties of any course, but, as far as my experience goes, it is always blowing hard at Westward Ho!   I am told that when Braid did his 69, he had a still day, and I certainly believe it, for the reason that no human man could play such a round in a high wind; it is almost incredibly good in a dead calm.   Person-ally, however, I have never found anything but a fine fresh wind blowing, a wind from the west that causes one to slice woefully on the way out and hook horribly on the way home.   I revisited Westward Ho! after a lamentably long absence of some ten years, and found the same wind still blowing, and it brought vividly back to me the recol-lections of how for one solid week I had sliced my tee-shots twice daily at the fourth, fifth, sixth, and seventh holes.

No course ever had more convincing testimony paid to its difficulties than did Westward Ho! at that Easter of slicing memory in 1900.   There was a team of the Royal Liverpool Club with Mr. Hilton to lead it—Mr. Ball and Mr. Graham were not there; there was a strong team of the Oxford and Cambridge Golfing Society; and there were all the local champions. Yet out of that field Mr. Horace Hutchinson won the Kashmir Cup with a score of 179, which represents, unless my arithmetic be at fault, but one under an average of five strokes a hole. It was in truth the most desperately difficult golf, and there was but one player who seemed able to triumph over it. That was the late Mr. J. A. T. Bramston, then a freshman at Oxford, who for the first time showed the world in general what a magnificent golfer he was. He played in four team matches against the most redoubtable opponents, and beat them all. He beat Mr. Hutchinson by a number of holes so large that it would be kinder to draw a discreet veil over the details, and Mr. John Low by a smaller but still very sufficient margin. Mr. Hilton and Mr. Humphrey Ellis (then at his very best, and how terribly good that best was!) he defeated by some two or three holes apiece. It was the most brilliant week in a brilliant and all too short career.

If Westward Ho! was difficult then—albeit with a gutty ball—how difficult must it be now, when Mr. Fowler has stretched it and bunkered it, so that there are some ready to rise up and call him not blessed. The one alleviation is that the rushes have been cut away in a good many places, and though bunkers have replaced them, no bunker is so fatal as a Westward Ho! rush, which is as tall as the golfer himself, and a great deal stronger. Practically the only criticism now to be made is in its essence a futile one, namely, that it is a pity that providence did not see fit to bring the true sandy golfing country up to the club-house door, instead of interposing that short stretch of low-lying and rather depressing marshland.

There the marsh is, however, and the best has undoubtedly been made of it, so that the first three and the last two holes, if they have no particular fascination, are thoroughly good and difficult : more difficult, indeed, than some of the more attractive ones. The first hole demands two very long, straight shots, for there is a ditch to catch a slice and only a narrow opening to the green. The second, again, is a fine, long driving hole, a little 'dog-legged' in character, and at the third, which is a short one, the green is beleaguered with pot-bunkers on every side. Yet this third hole shows that there are limits to what human ingenuity can do, for the hole is as difficult as can be, and yet of so flat and melancholy an appearance that one could scarcely feel any warm affection for it.

By this time we are close to the famous 'Pebble Ridge,' and the real golfing country begins with the fourth hole, a fine two-shot hole with a well-guarded green. Next comes the fifth, and in front of the tee there is a bunker so colossal that the carry looks at first sight to be impossible. A good long carry it certainly is, but it is not nearly so appalling as it looks; a well struck ball will career gaily over it, and, if we feel frightened, we can make the carry a little shorter by going to the right. A moderate pitch will take us home after the drive, and this is true not only of the fifth, but of the sixth and seventh also.

It is just a little unfortunate that these holes, which have a good many features in common, should come so close together, for their doing so imparts just a suspicion of weakness to this part of the course. In each case there is a stirring tee-shot from a high tee, and if that be well struck we may then pitch easily home, although the greens are very well protected, and should have a comfortable string of fours. There is a spot further on among the hills to the left where some desire that the green should be placed, and if ever it is done, not only the sixth but indirectly the fifth and seventh will also be benefitted.

The eighth is an interesting little short hole—an ex- tremely difficult one from the back tee—and after that come two of the finest holes in golf, the ninth and tenth.

The ninth green lies in a hollow on the top of a small plateau at the range of two very full shots from the tee, and the superlative virtue of the hole consists in a little unobtrusive pot-bunker, before alluded to, in the face of the hill. We can hardly hope to drive far enough to carry the bunker in our second, and if we could it would scarcely be possible to stay on the green. Therefore, we must drive well out to the right, and hope to reach the green with a subtle hook. The ground breaks in towards the hole from the right, and so a perfectly played shot, with just sufficient hook, will keep turning and turning towards the hole, till it totters with its last gasp down the last slope and lies close to the hole. Often, of course, it will be out of the question to get home in two, but the hole will still be interesting, and our approach shot anything but a simple one.

The tenth affords a standing example of what a 'dog-legged' hole should be, and it is here that we come really to close quarters with the rushes. There is a vast tract of them in front of the tee, and if we could carry some three hundred and more yards no doubt we could reach the green in one. Assuming, however, that our driving powers are more limited, we drive well out to the right, carrying just as many yards of rushes as we safely dare; then, turning to the left, we play our second between the rushes on one side and rough country on the other over a bunker and on to a narrow gully of a green. With a favourable wind we may hope to get home easily enough with an iron, but when two really full shots are needed, it is a hole for gods and heroes.

Next we come to some of the new holes. At the eleventh we drive not over but down an avenue of rushes, and must then play a shot which is curiously rare at Westward Ho!—a high, quickly stopping pitch over a cross-bunker. The twelfth and thirteenth are both good two-shot holes, the former, with a green most sternly bunkered, and the latter, with a lovely little plateau green. This plateau looks so eminently natural that I have once fallen into the error of describing it as such, thereby doing grave injustice to Mr. Fowler, who built it in the middle of a flat plain.

Fourteen is a short hole with a bunker in front and rushes in the neighbourhood: a good hole, but comparatively ordinary, and certainly not so attractive as the other short hole, the sixteenth. This is but the length of a mashie pitch, but what a difficult pitch it is! When I last played it the wind blew strongly from left to right, and the inhuman green-keeper had cut the hole in the left-hand corner of the green. To pitch right up to the hole was to run far over the green; to be at all short meant a pot-bunker, while a ball with the least suspicion of cut would tear away to the right and end, in all probability, in another bunker. It seemed to be almost necessary to pitch on a particular bump, on a particular hill just short of the flag— a desperate task.

I must go back for a minute to praise the fifteenth, a hole which has the added interest of alternative routes, according as we drive to right or left of a formidable hedge of furze, and then we come to a parlous long hole, the seventeenth. There is a ditch guarding the green, but before we arrive at the approaching stage, we must hit first of all a good tee-shot, and then a good brassey shot, over a rampart of terrible appearance. This is the one bunker on the course which is, from an artistic point of view, unworthy of it. It does indeed look as if it had been transplanted from some inland park, but do not let us be too hard on it, for there is much joy in the carrying of it.

At the last hole we should, with a good second shot, carry the burn and get a four, but there is a gentleman waiting with a net to fish our ball out if we fail, and the sight of him is apt to have a horribly destructive effect. If we go into the burn we shall be reminded of the fact when we are paying for our caddie, by the demand for the recognized toll of one penny for its rescue. Finally, no account of Westward Ho! would be complete without

76

a reference to the tea at the club-house. There is a particular form of roll cut in half and liberally plastered with Devonshire cream and jam. Epithets fail me, and I can only declare that the tea is worthy of the golf.

From Westward Ho! we may cross the border into Cornwall, a thing infinitely more easy to do in the imagination than in a train. Cornwall has several pleasant courses —Newquay, Lelant, St. Enodoc, and Bude, amongst others. Of these, St. Enodoc is a course of wonderful natural possibilities, and for that matter there is a rather solitary, inaccessible piece of land near Hale, not far from Lelant, where might be made one of *the* golf courses of the world. So at least it seemed to me as I wandered once on a Sunday morning amongst its hills and valleys.

Bude is a place beloved by many summer visitors, and the course is a good course if there are not too many of them upon it. The turf is of the seaside order, and there are many hills that must once have been sandhills, so that perhaps in some earlier geological epoch the course might have been more exciting than it is now. These hills are now, for the most part, covered with grass, but the sand appears quickly enough if a bunker has to be cut. There is one fact which is perhaps a little sad about Bude, and that is, that though there are the most magnificent waves to be seen there, the golf course is not the place to see them from, and we do not really catch sight of them till we come to the sixteenth hole, which a friend of mine has christened the 'Nursery Maid' hole. Here we have to play across a road that leads inland from the beach, and, as we are often finishing our round at precisely the same moment when the nurserymaids are conducting their young charges in for lunch, it becomes necessary to wait while an apparently endless procession wends its way homeward with much purposeless halting of children and screaming of maids.

Perhaps the best hole on the outward journey is the third, where there are really a variety of reasons why we should very likely play a bad second shot. In the first place, we shall not improbably have rather a hanging lie from which to play our pitch, and, to make things more difficult, the green is sloping away from us. Guarding the green is a fine natural bunker, where the punishment is apt to be very severe, and beyond it is a sandy road, so that altogether our pitch cannot possibly be called easy. We can so place our tee-shot as to modify its terrors, but we can by no means do away with them altogether.

After the agonies of the third there is a partial relapse into mildness, but there are good carries from the sixth and seventh tees; at the latter of the two over a big hill, the face of which has been cut out and converted into a bunker. The ninth too has a good tee-shot over another big bunker on to a green which is well protected on every side. At the tenth a punchbowl green brings hopes of a perhaps undeserved three, and then for a space we play in and out of some land that was once a garden or orchard: we can still see where the wall and the ditch used to run. We enter the garden by means of a good cleek shot over a big hill thickly covered with bents; leave it at the twelfth and

BUDE

The 'Nursery Maid' hole

re-enter it at the thirteenth, a hole not unlike the eleventh. At the fourteenth we may break the windows in a terrace of houses by a well executed slice; and at the sixteenth the aforesaid nurserymaids have to be circumvented. When we have paid for the windows and buried the nursery-maids, we play quite a short but deceptive iron shot to the seventeenth, avoiding a bunker and a sandy road, and so home with a good two-shot hole to end with.

We can go no further west than Cornwall, so let us turn back to **Burnham,** in Somersetshire. Whenever a golfing conversation turns upon blind holes, and one party boasts of the giant hills and deep valleys of any particular course, it is almost certain that another will say, "Ah, but you should just see Burnham in Somerset." Thus it happens that we go there for our first visit in the frame of mind of one who sets out for the Alps after having seen nothing perceptibly higher than Constitution Hill.

A first glance at the course assures us that we shall not be disappointed, for as we take our stand upon the tee we are ringed round with sandhills, and wherever the first hole may be, this much is evident, that we shall have to drive the ball over a mountain in order to get there. Hole succeeds hole, and still the endless range of hills goes on, and from the summit of each one we get the most lovely views : to the right a chain of hills, with the Cheddar Gorge in the distance; to the left the Bristol Channel, with the islands of Steep Home and Flat Home and an expanse of dim country on the other side. When we turn for home at the ninth, we still see the sandhills stretching tumultuously away towards Weston, with their strange fantastic shapes, and occasionally a narrow, meandering ribbon of turf in between. There seems to be material for at least one other course, and, indeed, the difficulty would appear to be not to find bunkers, but to find an open place where there are not too many of them.

With this wonderful stretch of country to work upon, it is small wonder that those who originally designed the course made a number of blind holes. They would have been hard put to it to do anything else, and there are, in fact, on the old course, if my reckoning be correct, no less than six blind one-shot holes, to say nothing of several longer holes, where the approach shot is played merely at a guide flag waving upon a hill top. I say the old course because, as I write, Burnham is in a transition stage, and what may be called the new course is practically in working order. Thus some of the blind short holes will disappear for ever, not, perhaps, without leaving a pang of regret behind them, and in their place come some flatter, and longer, and more open holes, which are not so characteristic of Burnham, but are none the worse for that. The hills will be all the more enjoyable when occasionally contrasted with the plains, and these new holes now give the course just that extra length that it needed.

Now let us play in imagination over the course in its altered condition, and tee up our ball for the first hole. There is a little dip between two grassy hills—a horribly narrow one it looks—and that is where we have to drive. A really fine shot may take us to the edge of the green,

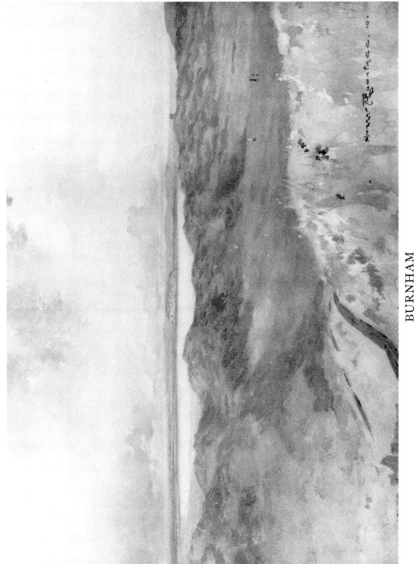

BURNHAM

Among the sandhills

and we may go on our way rejoicing with a three, for the green is big and good. A drive and a pitch in the country of hills should suffice for the second, and then come two excellent holes, where we cease to drive over the hills, and are set the far severer task of hitting straight down the gully that lies between them.

"This reminds me very much of Wallasey," I remarked, not without hopes of having made an interesting and original comment, and my guide answered in a tone, in which courtesy struggled with weariness, that he had often heard the same comment made before. Of these two holes the fourth, which is 'dog-legged,' and gives a well-deserved advantage to the fearless hitter, is particularly good; and then there comes a most fascinating hole, the fifth. Two full shots are needed, over some very broken and billowy country, to reach a green that lies at the bottom of a deep hollow. This hollow has merits, which are not given to all of its kind, for its sides are abruptly precipitous and not possessed of those gentle and flattering slopes, which coax the indifferently struck ball in the direction of the hole. The sixth, on the other hand, which is a one-shot hole, has all the vices which the fifth avoids, for here all roads lead to the flag, and the perfect shot, the paltry slice, and the too vigorous hook, may all meet together at such a range from the hole that a two is by no means improbable.

After being unduly pampered by this sixth hole, we are brought face to face with the sterner realities of life, and must be prepared to play a series of long and accurate brassey shots if we are to do anything better than five for each of the next three holes. Of these three the eighth and ninth are new, and the only thing to be said against them is that there is such a family likeness between them that it is a pity they come immediately together. Nothing but long, straight hitting will do here along a narrow tongue of grass that is flanked on either side by sand and bents.

The tenth deserves a special word, if only for the fact that a huge sandhill has had its head cut off—this is regarded as quite a minor operation at Burnham—in order that we may see the flag from the tee. There it is, a terribly long way off, as it seems, but one really good shot should reach the green, avoiding some little nests of pot-bunkers on the way, and there is a three to reduce the average of fives for the homeward journey. Another three should come at the twelfth, when only a short pitch is needed, but eleven and thirteen are very likely to be fives; long, narrow, flat holes, with broken ground and little clumps of rushes that are intensely business-like. The fourteenth is, I think, almost the best hole on the course, and certainly the tee-shot is the most alarming. We can see all our troubles only too clearly here—a sandy road full of the deepest ruts on the right, called in spirit of ostentatious levity the 'Old Kent Road,' and on the left a prickly and seductive hedge. If only there was a mountain in the way at this hole, we should probably come less frequently to grief. As it is, we concentrate all our attention on being straight, and are all the more terribly crooked in consequence.

The next two holes both need accurate approach shots,

and then comes the last and best of the blind holes, 'Majuba.' There is a steep hill of a rather curious conical shape to drive over, but the chief of the dangers lie on the far side, where the green lies in a narrow little gorge between a bunker on the right, and on the left a hill thickly covered with bents. This is as good a blind short hole as one could possibly wish for, and makes a sufficiently critical and exciting seventeenth, while the new eighteenth should be one of the best last holes to be seen anywhere. Two raking shots will be wanted, and the second of them, if it go as straight as an arrow between two flanking bunkers, will be rewarded by as good a piece of turf as the heart of the putter can desire.

Still travelling back in an easterly direction, we come to Broadstone, in Dorsetshire, not far from Bournemouth. **Broadstone** is, I think, rather an easy course to remember, which is the same as saying that the holes have each got very definite characters of their own; at any rate, although I have seen them but once, I can play them all quite clearly in my mind's eye, save only the park holes, which, truth to tell, are not much worth remembering. These park holes are certainly one of the drawbacks to the course. For six holes we are playing excellent golf in the right golfing country, with heather, and sand, and everything as it should be. Then we go through a wicket gate, the whole scene instantly changes, and, behold! we are playing a hole of the typical inland kind. There is no heather and no sand, save such as has been transplanted to fill up a number of conscientious little bunkers, and it is no great injustice to liken the turf to that of a good smooth field. For six holes we are playing in the park, and then the tyranny is overpast, and we emerge once more upon the heather for the rest of the round. In fact, the course is divided into three slices of six holes each, the first and last slice being good, and the middle slice being of very ordinary stuff indeed.

It is a little hard to understand why these park holes were ever made, because there is a glorious and apparently illimitable tract of heather waiting to be played over, only divided from the course by the railway. I believe there is a scheme afoot to make some further holes upon this heather, that is now so lamentably wasting its sweetness, and if this is done, Broadstone should be able to hold its head very high among inland courses.

In point of mere looks, it is very hard to beat now, and especially is there a most lovely view, with Poole Harbour in the distance, from the fifteenth hole, which is on the highest part of the course. This hole has likewise a unique feature in the shape of a genuine Roman tumulus, which at first sight the stranger is apt to attribute to the genius of Mr. Herbert Fowler, or some other maker of hazards. It stands almost exactly in the middle of the fairway, and those who drive too straight must deal with the situation as best they can with their niblicks.

A vast deal of trouble and money must have been spent on the putting greens, which are very smooth and good, and enormously big. They are, in fact, too big, and a revolutionary leader who should dig bunkers in the edge

BROADSTONE

The fourth hole

of them would be doing the course a service. I cannot help thinking, also, that rather too many of them are upon plateaus—not the plateaus of St. Andrews, but the plateau that is cut out of the side of a slope and has a back wall to cover a multitude of approaching sins. The bunkering in something of a patchwork, in which the theories of two opposite schools have been blended. We see, first of all, the remains of an older civilization in the shape of deep sandy trenches, with the accompanying ramparts dug right across the course. Then, as golfing opinion has progressed, or at any rate altered, there have been added, under Mr. Fowler's guidance, a good number of pot-bunkers, which seem to have some of the qualities of those we know and fear at Walton Heath, being easy to get into and hard to get out of. Besides these, the heather is always there to trap us at the sides of the course; there are also trees in places, and likewise whins, while one of the park holes so far demeans itself as to be guarded by an ordinary hedge.

The course begins very well with a fine, long, two-shot hole, a little 'dog-legged,' where the second shot will just creep on to the green between two sentinel bunkers. The second is another fine one, save that the plateau green has a terribly steep bank; and the third is wholly admirable, with its cheerful tee-shot from a height, followed by an iron shot down the middle of an avenue of trees. The fourth I believe to be likewise an excellent hole, but my attention was distracted from the hole by the scene I witnessed on the tee. There was an irascible gentleman and a small caddie; the caddie had made an inefficient tee, and the irascible gentleman was the possessor of a prolonged and solemn waggle. The waggle began and the ball fell off; the irascible gentleman made opprobrious remarks, and put it on the tee again, while the small caddie showed a dreadful tendency to laugh, which he restrained with obvious difficulty. This happened really innumerable times, till both the gentleman and the small boy appeared certain, from different causes, to die of apoplexy, and, indeed, I had serious fears for myself. The ball was ultimately despatched into a neighbouring ditch, and I passed on without having disgraced myself, but remembering very little about the hole. Both the fifth and sixth are short holes, though the sixth needs a long, straight shot, and then we pass into the park, or better still, by a short cut along the high road, which brings us back to the heathery country and the thirteenth hole—a good short hole, where a wood to the right of the green has doubtless slain its tens of thousands.

At the fourteenth we need a long, straight drive, followed by an iron shot that must be played firmly and boldly home on to a plateau guarded in front by a steep and unclimbable bank, and to the right by a pit of destruction, where the horrors of sand and whins are intermingled. Of the remaining holes, the seventeenth and eighteenth are both good, especially the former, which, with its tee-shot among the whins, has an air of Huntercombe about it. The sixteenth, however, does not seem at all worthy of its fellows, being, as it appeared to me, as essentially vicious as a hole can be. The ball is struck—with a measure of straightness, I admit—to the brow of a hill, then the hill does the rest. The ball hops, and skips, and jumps down the slope till it reaches a green built out from the hillside, and, lest it should jump too far and run over, there is a back wall of wire-netting. This is the kind of hole—I can think of nothing worse to say of it—that some people call 'sporting.'

Having given relief to my pent-up feelings on the subject of that sixteenth hole, I feel entirely at peace with Broadstone, which has some really fine holes, and is as pleasant a spot to play golf in—as breezy, and pretty, and quiet—as anyone could desire.

Besides Broadstone and the new course at Parkstone, which can be reached by a very short train journey, Bournemouth has two courses of its very own, Meyrick Park and Queen's Park. Both are situated in very pretty spots, amid the fir trees that are always with us at Bournemouth. **Meyrick Park** is rather a miniature affair, although it is not so short as when Tom Dunn originally laid it out. Then there was one green that could be reached with a shortish putt from the tee, and the most decrepit might hope for a round under eighty. There are still many threes for the accurate iron player, but there are also one or two good long holes, particularly the ninth, where we play, as it were, into the narrow neck of a bottle among the pinewoods. It is not unamusing, but the serious golfer will rather betake himself to the newer course at the Boscombe end of the world, **Queen's Park**. Both these courses belong to the Corporation, and all we have to do is to pay our shilling and play our round. We get plenty for our money at Queen's Park, for the course is over 6000 yards in length, which is certainly not too short for the wants of old gentlemen who totter round it.

It is really good golfing country, with big, rolling undulations and plenty of heather and sand. There are long, narrow gullies running in between the hills, rather reminiscent of another very pretty course, Hindhead. For the most part, however, we are not playing along the gullies, which would have tested our accuracy to the full, but rather go leaping from one hillside to the other; in fact, if we are virtuous we are always on a hill, and the valleys represent the infernal regions—it is only the wicked who go down into them. This is just a little monotonous, and we might rashly call it a fault in architecture. There is, however, a reason for it, in that all the best soil is to be found in the highlands, while the low-lying ground is in that respect unsatisfactory.

The course is still comparatively young, and has not yet put forth any very thick crop of bunkers; but the heather is wiry and tenacious and the fairway narrow. There are two consecutive holes of a most paralyzing narrowness— the seventh and eighth—where the ball has to be steered between a fir wood on the right and a high road, which is out of bounds, on the left. The third hole, again, is a fine two-shot hole, and there are plenty more. They are perhaps rather too similar in character owing to the recurring valleys, but they one and all need good play.

QUEEN'S PARK, BOURNEMOUTH

The eleventh green and twelfth tee

THE WEST AND SOUTH-WEST

Even among the heathery courses, which are nearly all good to look upon, Queen's Park takes a very high place for beauty, and it is a joy to find anything so pretty and peaceful on the very edge of a big town. Every prospect pleases, and only the old colonel, who is in front of us and plays fifteen more with his niblick, is entirely vile.

The reader must now make in imagination the short and generally innocuous crossing to the Isle of Wight, in order to see one of the most charming of nine-hole courses at **Bembridge.** The Royal Isle of Wight Golf Club can boast of a comparatively hoary antiquity, since it was founded in 1882, and Bembridge was perhaps rather more famous when there were fewer links in existence. It is still, however, very good golf, and has many faithful and affectionate friends. The nine holes dodge in and out after the manner of a cat's cradle, so that Bembridge has earned a reputation for being one of the most dangerous courses in the world, and it used to be said that all the local players expected to be hit once at least in the course of a year. To cry a brisk 'fore' is to absolve oneself from responsibility, and one may then let fly at any impeding player with a clear conscience. There is one particularly perilous spot, where the ball is apt to lie after a straight drive of moderate length on the way to the first hole. Here the player is in the midst of a veritable ring of death, since a hot fire may be opened upon him simultaneously from the seventh, eighth, and ninth tees, to say nothing of the first tee to his immediate rear. It is perhaps owing to this exciting characteristic of the course that that pleasant anachronism, the red coat, is still occasionally to be seen at Bembridge.

The course lies upon a spur of land between Bembridge harbour and the Solent, and one is rowed over to it from the hotel in a boat. Small things remain absurdly graven on the memory, and I remember nothing at Bembridge more clearly than the nautical gentleman who used to row us over a great many years ago, and his expression when Mr. John Low genially hailed him as "You licensed brigand." Once the stranger arrives on the course he will be struck, possibly by a ball, and certainly by the ubiquitous character of a road which winds about the course like a snake, and is an almost ever-present menace throughout the round; indeed, it has some say in the matter at every one of the holes, save only the third and the fifth. Some of its glory— or its horror, according to the light in which we view the matter—has, however, departed, for whereas it was once uniformly sandy and soft and full of the direst ruts, it is now metalled in many places, and so is naturally much less terrible. Another feature of the course, which is now less pronounced than it used to be, is the luxuriant growth of whins. These have become sadly thinner, and one who knows and loves his Bembridge well tells me that this is in a measure due to the havoc wrought among them in the early days of the rubber-cored ball, when a Haskell was infinitely precious and was not to be given up for lost till the entire neighbourhood had been laid waste with the niblick.

The first hole is one of the best on the course, requiring

BEMBRIDGE

A loop of the 'cat's cradle'

a drive, followed by an accurate cleek-shot on a still day, and against the wind two really fine shots. The whins lie in wait for a sliced shot, while on the left is the strong shore of the harbour. There is a delightful account of a round at Bembridge, written years ago by Mr. Horace Hutchinson, in which the writer pulls his shot at this hole on to the beach, and ultimately finds his ball lying upon a 'dead and derelict dog'—a grisly and, I trust, an unusual hazard. The next two holes are of very similar length, and can both be reached with a drive and a pitching shot; there are whins and a big bunker to trap the erring tee-shot, and in both cases the approach has to be played on to a green which is difficult to the verge of trickiness.

The fourth is a really good hole, some 460 yards in length, and has a thoroughly difficult tee-shot, since the most contemptible of golfing vices will be punished by a large bunker, while the more manly but still reprehensible pull lands the ball in a grassy pit. The fifth is a short hole, gifted with no particular merit and a number of whin bushes, but at the sixth we come to a hole which can hold its own in the very best of company. It has the virtue of presenting to the player the choice of two alternative routes, so that, according as he is long or short, courageous or cautious, he can vary the length of the hole for himself. If he is a strong and ambitious hitter, he will go straight for the second green, carrying the road on the way; the situation is the more poignant because the road is here not metalled, and failure must entail a measure of disaster. On the other hand, if the road be safely carried, he is left with a comparatively short and straightforward second shot, though he has still to cross a bunker of magnificent proportions that guards the green. The more careful, on the other hand, push their tee-shot to a spot further out to the right and short of the road, whence it is still possible to get home, but only by means of a shot that is both longer and harder. There are, I believe, many persons of sound judgment who think that the playing of the tee-shot on to the second green should be prohibited by law, both because all unnecessary risks of doing murder are undesirable and also on the ground that the second stroke by the right-hand line is more difficult and more interesting. Two holes of the drive and pitch type follow; indeed, a strong hitter may hope, under very favourable conditions, to get home with his tee-shot; but at the eighth in particular the drive must be a very straight one, for there are whins to right and left, and our old enemy the road lurks at the edge of the green. Finally, the green is a very tricky one, and altogether discretion at this hole lives fully up to its proverbial characteristics.

At the last hole, which calls for a drive and a good full iron-shot, a four is never to be despised, and with that we start off once more between the whins and the beach, and pass pale and trembling again through the fiery zone. The golf at Bembridge is most certainly attractive, and that it has other and more sterling qualities is shown by the fine players it has produced, the two Toogoods and Rowland Jones amongst them. "By their fruits ye shall know them" is true of golf links as well as of other things.

CHAPTER V.

EAST ANGLIA.

OF the many good courses in East Anglia, I have the tenderest and most sentimental association with **Felixstowe**, because it was there that I began to play golf. Till quite lately, however, I had not seen the course for a very long while, and my recollections of it were those of a small boy of eight or nine years old. The small boy wore a flannel shirt, brown holland knickerbockers, and bare legs, from which the sun had removed nearly all vestiges of skin. He used to dodge in and out among the crowd, hurriedly playing a hole here and there, and then waiting for unsympathetic grown-ups in red coats to pass him. Willy Fernie was the professional there in those days, and in the zenith of his fame; it was not long before that he had beaten Bob Ferguson for the championship by holing a long putt for a two at the last hole at Musselburgh. Occasionally also another great golfer, Mr. Mure Fergusson, would come down from London to shed the light of his countenance upon the course and be breathlessly admired by the small boy from a respectful distance.

GOLF COURSES

As far as I can remember, my best score then was 70 for one round of the nine-hole course, and so I always pictured Felixstowe to myself as possessing longer holes and bunkers infinitely more terrible than those to be found on any other course. Felixstowe revisited appeared naturally enough to have shrunk a little; the Martello tower that stands on the edge of the first green is not quite so tall as I had pictured it, and some of the holes are quite short, but I still found it one of the most charming and interesting of courses. I came back to it on one of the most perfect of winter golfing days, with the sun shining on the sea and the red roofs of Baudsey in the distance; it was a day to accentuate every romantic feeling, and it was with a perceptible thrill that I teed my ball in front of the very modest bunker, the carrying of which had once been among my wildest dreams.

As far as I could see, the course was almost exactly the same as it always had been. One or two of the bunkers had been rather more abruptly 'faced' with walls of turf; and the little hut, which once served Fernie for a shop, and whence he used to issue in a white apron and with a half-made club in his hand, had become a ladies' club-house; but otherwise the whole nine holes appeared entirely unchanged. Their names came back to me as I played them—the 'Gate,' the 'Tower,' 'Eastward Ho!' 'Bunker's Hill,' the 'Point'—and the only thing as to which I felt doubtful was the position of a certain bunker that used once to be known as 'Morley's Grave,' and was faced, if I remember rightly, with black timbers that have now vanished.

94

FELIXSTOWE

General view of the course

EAST ANGLIA

Looking at the course as impartially as possible, it seems to me now to possess a striking mixture of very easy and extremely difficult shots.   There are several tee-shots, for instance, where one may hit out in a very gay and careless spirit and with but the very smallest fear of disaster; there are other shots, and especially second shots up to the greens, where the ball has to be played to a very exact spot, and where no other spot will do.   The thing, however, that in a great degree makes the golf at Felixstowe is the truly magnificent finish.   With a breeze against the player, as it was when I was there, it is hard to conceive two more splendid and exacting holes than the eighth and ninth, 'Bunker's Hill' and the 'Point,' and—here is one of the advantages of a nine-hole course—we have to battle with them four times in one day's golf.   At the risk of exaggerating, I will boldy assert that I have never seen two such fine holes coming consecutively at the end of any golf course.

Those two I will keep till their proper place, and we will begin at the first with a drive over a sandy hollow into open country.   A bad slice may see us labouring upon the sea-shore, but if we keep well to the left there is no great difficulty, and a firm pitch over a cross-bunker should land us safely on a big open green—it is, in fact, a double green—between the hut and the Martello tower.   The second, or 'Gate,' is a short hole with a very billowy green; indeed, one little valley, in which the hole is sometimes placed, is shaped for all the world like a horse trough, and the ball will always come rolling back from its steep sides, and must almost infallibly end very near the hole. After this come three thoroughly good two-shot holes—the 'Bank,' the 'Tower,' and 'Bent Hills'—at all three of which the tee-shot is quite easy, and the second shot both interesting and difficult; at both the fourth and fifth there is an old-fashioned, honest cross-bunker, which has to be carried if we are to get near the hole, and if the wind is adverse and the ground slow, nothing but a really good brassey shot will suffice. At the sixth—'Eastward Ho!'—a drive and a running shot with the iron takes us close up to Baudsey Ferry and another Martello tower, and then we turn homeward for the 'Ridge'—a drive and a short pitch; at both these holes we should be hoping and trying for threes, and they are neither of them possessed of any particular difficulty. So far we may have done very well, and our score should not greatly exceed an average of fours, but now comes Bunker's Hill, to be played, as we will imagine, against a fair breeze. The drive is comparatively simple, but for the second we must hit a very full shot as straight as an arrow; the green is quite a small one, guarded on the right by a road and a wilderness of thick grass beyond, while in front and to the left is sand in abundance. To play short is the act of a coward, and there will be a certain splendour even in our failure, for it will be failure on a grand and expensive scale. This is true, even in a greater degree, of the 'Point,' a hole that must have wrecked the hopes of many a prospective medal winner; nay, there cannot be such a thing as a prospective medal winner at Felixstowe till he has played the second shot to the Point for the second time. There is some chance of trouble from the tee, for besides the bunker immediately in front, there is a long tongue of sand that stretches inwards from the road at such a distance that it may well catch a fairly well-struck ball. We will assume, however, that we are safely on the crest of the hill, with the ball neither very far above or below us—this latter a considerable assumption. The flag is fluttering in the distance close to the first tee at the range of an absolutely full shot, and on the very narrowest, most tapering strath imaginable. To the right is a field, which is out of bounds; to the left is a hollow of broken, sandy country; close to the hole is the seashore, but that we shall hardly reach against the wind. Here, if our score be good or our adversary in trouble, we may play short without much shame, but even so we shall have to play very short and very accurately, and the third shot will not be without peril. It is a grand four—something more than a steady five, a likely six; really a tremendous hole with which to end. Everybody must long to go back to Felixstowe, solely in order to master the Point thoroughly, but they will never do it; it is a hole of such transcendent quality that is must beat us in the end.

There are four courses in Norfolk, which naturally divide themselves into two groups of near neighbours, Cromer and Sheringham, Brancaster and Hunstanton. The two former are of the type which may be not too respectfully denominated inland-super-mare. The sea is there, and very nice it looks. The courses are close to the sea—so close that they spend some of their time, especially at Cromer, in falling into it; but the turf is not the crisp and sandy turf of the links. It is the down turf, such as we find at Eastbourne or Brighton, very pleasant and springy to walk on, but—not quite the right thing. There is a considerable family likeness between the two courses. Both are situated on the top of a cliff; both have fine, bold sweeping undulations and hillsides dotted here and there with gorse bushes, and both are to a large extent dependent on the artificial bunker.

Cromer, like Felixstowe, makes me feel a very old golfer, because, when I first played there, there was a little ladies' course along the edge of the cliff, which has many, many years since toppled peacefully over into the German Ocean. Later on I saw an excellent seventeenth hole share the same fate, and I suppose the poor first hole must go the same way some time. It is particularly sad, because the holes on the down land near the cliff constitute the most attractive part of the course. The holes inland, which were added later, are long and well bunkered, and have doubtless all the Christian virtues, but they are just a little agricultural and uninspiring.

It is certainly to the old holes that the memory returns most fondly. The club-house stands in the bottom of a deep hollow, with hills rising pretty steeply out of it on three sides, and the first tee-shot has to be driven straight up a gully between two of them. Then comes a shot demanding the agility of a chamois and a maximum of local knowledge. With the left foot a good deal higher than the right we play an iron-shot into the distance, and if all goes

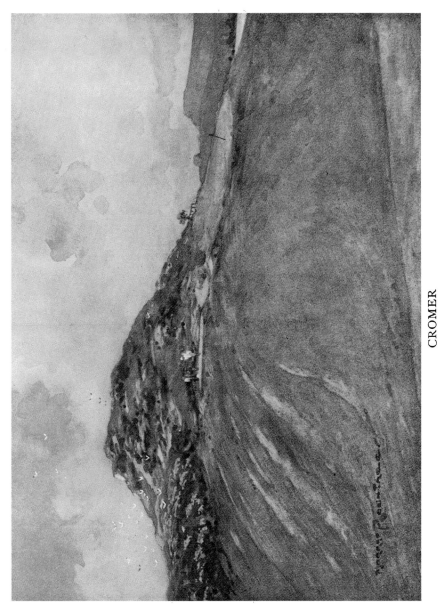

CROMER

The sixteenth tee

well, shall find the ball on a green which is walled in by cops and bunkers. If all goes ill, it is possible that we lose it over the cliff, but for such a disaster we shall need hooking powers of no mean order.

The third is another spirited hole, where we plunge down a steep hill between two lines of bracken to a green in the bottom of the valley. Then we retire to a vantage point on the left, and fire over the heads of our immediate successors on the putting green. After some little dodging about among gorse bushes, we dash down hill again—a very long way this time—and then play an adroit little pitch up to a plateau cut out of the face of the neighbouring mountain. Then we leave the nice down turf to pass for a while on to undisguisedly inland holes, which stretch away towards Overstrand. As I said before, there is nothing very thrilling about these holes, but we shall need good, honest flogging if we are to cope with them successfully. I prefer to come back to the sixteenth, which, with a strong wind blowing, as it not infrequently does, takes a great deal of playing. There is more plunging to be done—down into one valley with precipitous sides, then up a long hill, and finally on to a green that sits perched on the crest; there are also cross-bunkers, and there is bracken to the left and the mighty ocean to the right. Finally, for the last hole we drop down once more into the deep hollow from which we started our mountaineering. No more than a nice firm iron-shot is needed, and we shall be holing out in a comfortable three in front of the club-house; but the distance is infinitely deceitful, so much so that once—on the occasion of an exhibition match—Herd taking his brassey, and relying on the misleading advice of his caddy, carried not only the green, but the club-house as well.

From Cromer to Sheringham is but a few miles, and we may play a morning round on one course and an afternoon round at the other. At **Sheringham** we shall be called upon to do only a moderate amount of climbing and some of the very stoutest hitting with the brassey that has ever been required of us. The theory of the good-length hole has been carried almost to its ultimate limit there, and unless the wind be favourable and the ground uncommonly fast, cleeks and driving irons will be no manner of good to us. Strenuous punching with the brassey is the order of the day, and even so, unless we have been hitting the ball as clean as a whistle, we shall say to the long-suffering Mr. Janion, "Hang it all; you never ought to have put the tee back at the ninth hole. Braid himself with a Dreadnought could not get there in two."

Some of these two-shot holes at Sheringham are really of extraordinary splendour, and give the lie to those who say that with a rubber-cored ball golf is no longer an athletic exercise. There are the second and fourth, for example, which run parallel to one another, so that by no means can we hope to have the wind with us both ways. The fourth needs a particularly long second, for there is a deep cross-bunker in front of the green. It is just a little like the last hole at Muirfield, and we must pick the ball well up—no scuffling and scrambling will do—and hit a ball with a long, swooping carry that shall fall spent and lifeless on the green

SHERINGHAM

Out of bounds (on the way to the seventh hole)

beyond. After this hard work we are let down more easily, and a drive and a pitch should suffice at the fifth and sixth. The latter is a very attractive hole, with the most glorious tee-shot from a high hill, a fine view of the sea, and a fascinating approach-shot at the end, which we can pitch or run according as seems best to us.

At the eighth we carry a lifeboat house from the tee—an unique hazard in my experience—and play a long second shot full of interest and possible disaster. Then, alas! we have to leave the sea, which we have been keeping on our right-hand side, and go further inland. All the home-coming holes are good and difficult, but we miss the sea terribly. It is so pleasant to have it there as a reminder that we are really playing on a seaside course and not inland. The finish is a particularly good one, the seventeenth, especially against a breeze, being quite one of the best on the course, since there is a railway which terrifies us into a hook just when we must go straight if we are to get the requisite distance.

All this time I have been talking of nothing but long holes, and that is to do the course an injustice, for there are some very pleasant short ones. The third is a hole that one might expect to find at Hoylake—a pitch over the angle of a field, which is bounded by walls of turf; it is one of the remnants of the old nine-hole course, and therefore regarded with a jealous and quite justifiable affection. The greens are excellent throughout the course, and the number of people who drive off between sunrise and sunset on a summer's day shows that Sheringham does not suffer from a lack of popularity.

I should imagine that **Brancaster,** before golf was introduced there, must have been quite one of the quietest and most rural spots to be found in England. Even now it is wonderfully peaceful, and has a distinct charm and character of its own. We get out at Hunstanton Station, and drive a considerable number of miles along a nice, flat, dull east country road till we get to the tranquil little village, with a church and some pleasant trees and an exceedingly comfortable Dormy House. In front of the village is a stretch of grey-green marsh, and beyond the marsh is a range of sandhills, and that is where the golf is.

The great defect of Brancaster used to be the thinness and poverty of the turf. The holes were splendidly conceived, and the carries blood-curdling; but the sand was so near the surface that the lies were none of the best, and the putting greens sometimes of the worst. I retain a vivid recollection of a visit to Brancaster with a somewhat irascible friend. He greeted me at the Dormy House door with the depressing words:

"It's utterly impossible to play here. We had better take the next train back."

"Oh, no," I said cheerfully. "As we have come here, I think we had better play."

"Very well," he rejoined. "Of course, you won't mind putting with your niblick. A mashie is no good at all."

We stayed, and personally I enjoyed myself; I don't

BRANCASTER

The ninth green and tenth tee

think my friend did, and certainly the greens were of a surpassing vileness. All that is changed now, and by some miracle of industry the course is a velvety carpet, and the greens are as of the greens of Sandwich, with plenty of good, holding grass upon them. Good greens are all that Brancaster needed, and now it has got them. Perhaps there is one more thing needed, and that is a stout man with a spade to dig a few more bunkers; but that want, I believe, is in course of being or has actually been remedied by now.

In the days of the gutty it was most emphatically a driver's course, since nobody could get over the ground without exceptionally honest hitting. Even now, when the pampering Haskell has noticeably reduced its terrors, it is still a driver's course, in the sense that it is one on which one derives the maximum of sensual pleasure from opening one's shoulders for a wooden club shot. Moreover, long driving does pay—for the matter of that, it pays anywhere—because there are several second shots which are enormously more formidable, when they have to be played with something like a full shot. There is, for instance, the ninth—a hole of which men used to speak with the same reverential awe with which they alluded to the 'Maiden' at Sandwich. Certainly that bunker in front of the green is sufficiently desperate, and to be compelled to approach the hole with a brassey may well inspire fear, but a good drive on a calm day should leave us little more than a firm half-iron shot to play, and then we can afford to treat the bunker almost with contempt. The same remark applies in a

103

measure to the fourth hole, and likewise to the fourteenth. There are beautifully guarded greens and alarming bunkers, and just the extra yards gained by a good drive make a world of difference in easiness of the approach.

Few things are more terrifying than the first hole at Brancaster on a cold, raw, windy morning, when our wrists are stiff and our beautiful steely-shafted driver feels like a poker. There is a bunker—really a very big, deep bunker —right in front of our noses, and stretching away for a hundred yards or so, and the early morning 'founder' that would send the ball ricochetting away for miles at the first hole at Hoylake or St. Andrews brings us to immediate grief. There is nothing very thrilling about the second shot, and the next two holes, although good enough, must remain unsung. At the fourth, however, we come to a thoroughly entertaining hole; the second shot has to be played from a plain, over a hill, and on to something that one might call a plateau, were it not that such a term hardly does justice to the curliness of the green.

There is a fascinating little pitch over a kind of gorge, and on to another plateau for the fifth; but the hole on the way out is, I think, the eighth. There is nothing quite like it anywhere else, as far as I know. I can think of no better simile to describe it than that of a man crossing a stream by somewhat imperfect stepping-stones, so that he has to make a perilous leap from one to the other. There are, as it were, three tongues or spits of land; on the first is the tee, on the third is the green, and between them lie strips of marsh, a sandy waste on which we may get a good lie, but are infinitely more likely to get a bad one. There is a safe, conservative method of playing the hole, which consists of a second shot along the second tongue, followed by a hop over the marsh on to the green. On the other hand, there is a more dashing policy, whereby we go out for a big shot off the tee, and try to reach the third tongue in our second stroke. The first plan is reminiscent of the methods of Allan Robertson, who, we are told, used to play a certain hole at St. Andrews in three short spoon shots; the second belongs to the more daring methods of to-day. The wind, of course, has a great deal to say to our tactics, but, however we play the hole, we have got to hit all our shots as they should be hit, and that is as much as to say that the hole is a good one.

The ninth I have already spoken of, and with an adverse wind it is undoubtedly a magnificent hole. With the wind behind it becomes much more commonplace, but wherever the wind, we are not likely to be quite happy till we have left it behind in a scoring competition. In a match we may treat it cavalierly enough, and therefore successfully, but in a medal there is a chance of an overwhelming disaster as a punishment for just one bad shot. We may carry the bunker itself, and yet with a pull we may plunge into a hedge of brushwood or on to the seashore beyond it. We may be just short with our second—a matter of six inches perhaps—and we shall be battering the bunker's unyielding face till our card is shattered and wrecked. If a bunker be only big enough and bad enough, it is undeniably difficult to treat it with just the right admixture of contempt and respect.

The first few holes on the way home do not appear to me particularly thrilling, but when we get to the fourteenth there is a really good second to be played over a ghastly bunker on to a small well-guarded green. The sixteenth provides an ingenious example of the plateau hole, and there is a bunker that takes no denial guarding the home green.

Brancaster is like one or two other courses—Harlech and Sandwich are those that come into my mind. The golf is not desperately difficult golf if one is hitting the ball steadily into the air, but the occasional top which we may allow ourselves with something like impunity on more difficult courses spells ruin. If the punishment of the utterly bad shots was the aim and object of all golf, these three courses would be the best in the world. I don't think they are any of them quite as good as that, but they all provide the very jolliest of golf, and Brancaster is not the least jolly of the three.

Hunstanton is very amusing golf; it is more than that, for it is for the most part very good golf. Perhaps it is a little unfairly overshadowed in public estimation by its near neighbour Brancaster, which is altogether on rather a bigger and grander scale. Brancaster has the faults which are apt to go with its peculiar virtues; it gives the player just a little too much rope, an accusation that is not lightly to be made against Hunstanton. They had a visitation from Braid at Hunstanton a year or two back, and he left

HUNSTANTON

Under snow

a most destructive trail of bunkers behind him; wonderfully cunningly devised they are, so that if we narrowly avoid one we are very likely to be caught in another or 'covering' bunker, just as we were rejoicing at our unmerited escape.

The outgoing nine holes at Hunstanton are nearly all good; the home-coming half is much more unequal in quality. The last two holes always made a fine finish, but some of the preceding holes were once of rather poor quality. Braid's bunkers, however, and the stretching of tees, and a radical change at the thirteenth have worked wonders, and nowadays a low score at Hunstanton, though perfectly possible, has to be earned by sound and accurate golf.

We begin just as at Brancaster, with a most terrifying bunker to carry. It is a magnificent bunker and a very good one-shot hole, but these caverns in front of the nervous starter do most sadly retard progress on a crowded green. The second and third are really fine holes both of them, especially the second, which wants two good shots and a pitch, with accurate going all the way. The fifth demands two of the best shots to carry a cop in front of the green; there is, moreover, a chance of slicing into the river Hun. At the sixth we play a blind pitch into a kind of amphitheatre among sandhills—a hole which is picturesque but fluky; but at the eighth we come to a really fine hole—the best on the course—with a fine slashing second over the corner of a field that is out of bounds. It is a hole where we must decide on our own policy on the tee, and either go as close as may be to the field to begin with or else reluctantly put aside all our noblest ideals and play pawkily to the left for a five.

On the way home we have at the tenth an excellent and teasing tee-shot along one of those narrow necks which every 'architect' must long for, and a good eleventh as well. Then the course suffers rather a relapse, but the seventeenth and eighteenth are worth much fine gold. Certainly there is an element of luck about the lie off the tee-shot at the seventeenth, but if only we are lucky and the wind be not too strong against us, we can hit out manfully, and the ball will sail away over a hill and a prodigious big bunker in its face on to a nice big green. The last is even better, with its narrow and billowy green, guarded by a bunker in front, another to the right, and a horrid hard road to the left. If I add that I once did these two holes in consecutive threes it is not in a spirit of boasting, but merely to recall a sensation of exquisite bliss. Hunstanton is very good golf of the most genuine and sandy kind. If it is not in the highest class, it is at least agreeably near to it.

Now leaving Norfolk behind, we ought to see one course in Lincolnshire, that of the Seacroft Club at Skegness. **Skegness**, as is well known to everyone from Mr. Hassall's delightful poster, is 'so bracing,' and I would not for the world dispute the fact. I had, however, the misfortune to visit it on one of the most stifling days in July, when the whole flat expanse of Lincolnshire fen lay panting under a hot haze, and our progress round the links was quite unlike that of the gentleman depicted by Mr. Hassall, skimming buoyantly over the ground with a cooling sea breeze behind

SKEGNESS

The second shot at the ninth hole

him. If, therefore, I have pleasant recollections of Skegness, it must surely be a good course; and so it is, lacking,. I think, only one thing, a wind that blows from two places at once. It is one of those courses that runs, roughly speaking, straight out and home, and the nine holes that we play with the wind in our face we think really beautiful, while with the wind behind us we are just a little bit disappointed. This is, of course, only the impression of a casual visitor; and, moreover, it must often happen that wind is neither for us nor against us, but blows straight across the course. Then the golf must be really difficult, for the fairway is uniformly narrow and the rough wonderfully tenacious; indeed, I have only met with more clinging rough at Le Touquet, where is to be found a diabolical undergrowth, which the caddies call by the name of ' les épines,' and the golfers by a variety of epithets—all of them unprintable.

The course begins admirably with two narrow and difficult holes, where it is equally easy to heel the ball out of bounds or to hook it into the rough before described. The third is blind but exciting—a drive on to the top of a hog-backed ridge, followed by a little pitch over the brow of the hill on to a green in a dell. Of the other outgoing holes, the two best are perhaps those called respectively ' Spion Kop ' and ' Gibraltar,' and of these ' Gibraltar ' is the best. Here there is a really fine second shot to be played over a whole range of sandy mountains, and if, perhaps with some mistaken idea of making the ball rise quickly, we impart any cut to the ball, it sails away out of bounds, and we are left with the sandy mountains still uncrossed.

GOLF COURSES

'Gibraltar' is certainly the most memorable hole on the way out, and 'Sea View' strikes equal terror into the soul on the homeward journey. Here the hole stands on a small plateau, and in front is a big bunker in the face of the hill. With a wind behind we may hope to get home with a high, hard hit with an iron, but on a still day it must need the very best of brassey shots, and a shot, moreover, that shall soar high in the air and then fall comparatively straight to earth. Beyond the green is a waste of sand, and the hole lives up to its name, for there is a view of a big stretch of sea. The sixteenth is a 'dog-legged' hole that makes some demand upon our cunning, and we must hit long and straight along the bottom of a gully for the last two holes, so that the course ends as it began, very well.

Given straight hitting from the tee, we should return something better than a respectable score, but the demand for straightness is great, and, indeed, the constant avenues of rough remind one rather of the best of modern inland courses. It is genuine seaside golf, however, with good turf and plenty of sand, and the sea itself, although we do not often see it. Neither do we see—and this is an un-mixed blessing—the teeming swarms of trippers that come to Skegness to be braced.

CHAPTER VI.

THE COURSES OF CHESHIRE AND LANCASHIRE.

OF all the links in the north of England, **Hoylake** comes first on account of its historic traditions, the eminence of its golfing sons, and, as I think at least, its own intrinsic merits. At Hoylake the golfing pilgrim is emphatically on classic ground. As he steps out of the train that has brought him from Liverpool he will gaze with awe-struck eyes upon surroundings in which the irreverent might see nothing out of the ordinary.

"Perhaps it was here," he will muse, "that the youthful Johnny Ball once toddled to school, his satchel on his back. The infant Hilton may have been wheeled by his nurse upon these very paving stones. Nay, Jack Graham may even now, perchance, be seen at this identical station at which I have just got out of my train taking *his* train to go into Liverpool every morning."

By the time that these remarkable thoughts have flashed like lightning through his mind, the pilgrim will find himself wandering down a straight, dusty, unattractive road, which

111

is flanked by villas of a comfortable though prosaic appearance, and wondering where on earth this famous links can possibly be. Then he will discover that what he thought was another and particularly gorgeous villa was really the Royal Liverpool Club-house, and dashing upstairs, he will see out of the smoking-room window the famous links of Hoylake spread out beneath him.

On a first view they are not imposing. All that appears is a vast expanse cut up into squares and strips by certain cops or banks, partly walled in by roads and houses, with a range of sandhills in the far distance. Yet this place of dull and rather mean appearance is one of the most interesting and most difficult courses in the world, and preeminently one which is regarded with affection by all who know it well.

That the course is either interesting or difficult all will not agree, but those who disagree most loudly with the statement will, I venture to assert, usually be found to be the worst of players. "I call Hoylake a rotten course : there are no bunkers to get over; the fellow I was playing with topped all his tee-shots and never got into trouble." Such is a verdict often heard after a first visit to Hoylake. The critic should then further be asked his opinion of St. Andrews, and it will generally be found that he classes St. Andrews and Hoylake together as the two worst courses he has ever seen. He may forthwith be treated with silent contempt, and his opinions may be ignored. He has effectually written himself down an ass. What this person says is absolutely true; there are very few bunkers in front

112

HOYLAKE (1)

Looking out to Hilbre from the ninth tee

of the tee at Hoylake, and the man who tops his tee-shot does escape condign punishment more often than he would on a golf course designed on principles of perfect equity. Those short drives, however, though they do not plunge the culprit waist high in sand, bring their own penalty by making it practically impossible for him to reach the green in the right number of shots. Some of the holes that we are supposed to reach in two shots are desperately long, and with a top from the tee all hope is straightway gone. At least if Hoylake does not demand that the ball should always be hit into the air—a matter that is not after all of very great importance among the reasonably competent— it does make very exacting demands in the matter of length and straightness. How fiendishly narrow is the third hole, with that fatal cop on the left and rushes on the right. How we do have to press if we are to hit far enough at those last five holes—'Field,' 'Lake,' 'Dun,' 'Royal,' and the home hole; what splendid names they have, and what splendid finish they provide for a match—surely the most exhausting finish to be found on any links in the world.

Then, too, there is always a rich reward at Hoylake for the man who can play his approaches really straight and with a firm, sure touch. There are some courses where the greens are always helping us and the ball is always running to the hole. We may play a most indifferent iron shot on to the outskirts of the green, and behold! a kindly slope has intervened on our behalf, and the ball finishes within comfortable putting range. Hoylake is emphatically not one of those easy and enervating places; there the greens are always fighting against the player, and he must hold his shot straight on the pin from start to finish.   If he does not, the chances are that the ball will take a vindictive leap, and his next shot will still come under the category of approaching.   There is none of your smug smoothness and trimness about Hoylake; it is rather hard and bare and bumpy, and needs a man to conquer it.   The game, as I have said, is not made easy for us, and this is true—a little too true, alas! —of the putting greens.   Sometimes they are good enough, though hardly ever easy; but very often, unless I have been exceptionally unfortunate in my experience, they are rather rough and lumpy, and make the holing of short putts a very anxious business.   Time was when the greens were the particular pride of the course, and Mr. Hutchinson wrote in the Badminton Library that ''The links of Hoylake are associated, in the mind of every golfer who has played upon them, with the most perfect putting greens in all the world.'' Since that eulogy was written the building of houses and the consequent drainage operations are said to have drained some subtle and beautiful quality out of the greens, and they may now be said to form the weakness rather than the strength of the course.   Even now, however, they are not so rough as they often look, and the man who has a delicate and withal a fearless touch of his putter will still be rewarded at Hoylake.

One more good quality of the holes at Hoylake deserves a word of mention; it has been called by Mr. Low their 'indestructibleness.'   By this most useful, if inelegant, word, he means that they are good whether played with or against the wind, and that is very high praise, particularly as there are few courses on which a change of wind more completely alters the character of each individual hole. Blessed indeed is the hole which can keep its good character whichever way the wind is blowing.

The first hole is so good and difficult that it seems almost a pity that we are compelled to play it before we have got thoroughly into our stride. Whatever the wind, it is our duty to begin with a long, straight drive between the club-house railings on the left and a sandy ditch and cop on the right. At about the distance of a good drive from the tee the cop turns at a right angle to the right, and we must follow the cop, skirting it as near as we dare. The wind cannot be either with or against us for both our first and second shots, and we shall have a fine opportunity of showing our skill in the use of it. If it be blowing strongly against us on the tee we shall hardly get home in two, and our second must needs be played over the corner of the cop and the out-of-bounds region that lies within it. If it blow behind us we shall be well clear of the cop with our drive, and may hope to be home with a low, running second with an iron club, but it must be a parlous straight one. Altogether there are few finer holes to be found anywhere, and it would always find a place in my eclectic eighteen holes.

Passing over the second—good hole though it be—we come to an unpleasantly narrow one—the third or 'Long' hole. If the wind is blowing freshly behind us we may aspire to reach the green in two very long and very straight shots, but as a rule we shall require two drives and a pitch. Along the left-hand side runs a sandy ditch beneath a turf wall with absolutely precipitous sides, and woe betide the man whose ball lies tucked up hard under the face of that wall; he will be lucky if he can get it out backwards, forwards, or at all. I saw Mr. John Ball extricate himself from this predicament by an extraordinary stroke, or so it seemed to me. He stood on the top of the wall, far out of reach of the ball, then leaped down into the ditch, hitting as he jumped, and out came the ball most gallantly; it needs something more than local knowledge to play such a shot as this.

The fourth is a short hole—the 'Cop' by name, so called from yet another bank that guards it. Then follow two good two-shot holes, of which the sixth, or 'Briars,' has the distinction of having been halved in nine in the final of an amateur championship. The tee-shot must be struck straight and true over the angle of hedge, while anything in the nature of an attempt to sneak round by the right entails a prickly death among the whins. Safely over the hedge, we have yet two sandy trenches to carry, and the green is guarded by rushes and pot-bunkers, so that if nine be an excessive total, four is a comparatively small one. Next comes one of the finest short holes in the world, 'The Dowie,' which is not only very good, but really unique. There is a narrow triangular green, guarded on the right by some straggling rushes and on the left by an out-of-bounds field and a cop; there is likewise a pot-bunker in front. To hit quite straight at this hole is the feat of a hero,

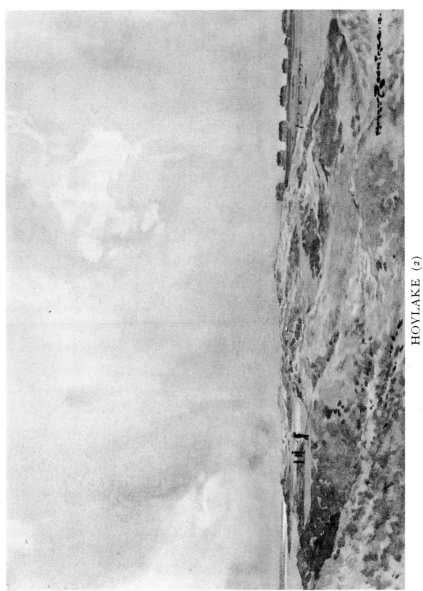

HOYLAKE (2)

The twelfth tee

for let the ball be ever so slightly pulled, and we shall infallibly be left playing our second shot from the tee. Nearly everybody slices at the Dowie out of pure fright, and is left with a tricky little running up shot on to the green. The perfect shot starts out of the right, just to show that it has no intention of going out of bounds, and then swings round with a delicious hook, struggles through the little rushy hollow, and so home on the green; it is a shot to dream of, but alas! seldom to play.

A long and reasonably narrow eighth hole takes us to the confines of West Kirby, and we turn our faces once more towards the club-house in the far distance. Two perfect shots that turn neither to the right nor to the left but keep down a narrow valley between two ranges of hills may see us safely on the ninth green, and we have reached the turn possibly, but by no means probably, in some 38 shots. The tenth is another longish hole of no particular features, but the eleventh hole consists of one big feature—the mighty Alps over which we must hit our very best shot if we are to gain a three. In the Amateur Championship of 1898 this hole was done in one in a rather singular way, the ball going full pitch into the bottom of the hole and staying there. The 'Hilbre' we may hope to reach with a drive and a cunning run up, and then we have a chance of another three at the 'Rushes.' Here we have nothing to do but play quite a short pitch over a cross-bunker and a little wilderness of rushes, but the hole is very close to the bunker, and the green is hard and full of unkind kicks, and a three is not to be despised. This is undoubtedly the last chance of a three we shall have, for from now onwards to the finish it will not be surprising if we have an uninterrupted run of fives. First comes the 'Field,' where the hole is most cunningly guarded by a triangle of rushes. A very respectable five is the 'Field,' and so is the 'Lake,' even if we go as straight as a die for the hole through 'Johnny Ball's Gap.' So again is the 'Dun,' where for two shots we have to keep clear of our old enemies, the cop and the sandy ditch, before playing a deft little pitch over a cross-bunker. At the 'Royal' we may hope for a four, since we have a fine wide expanse for the tee-shot, and a really accurate iron-shot should do the rest. There is plenty of room at the last hole again, but we shall need two absolutely clean-hit shots if we are to get home, and once more there is a cross-bunker in front of the green, at just such a distance from the hole that even if we get out in one we are likely to take three putts. And so at last we have finished those last five strenuous holes, and may go to the particularly excellent lunch provided by the Royal Liverpool Golf Club. They are not much to look at, those last five, but they are horribly good golf, and if you are only all square at the thirteenth with one of the Hoylake champions your chances of ultimate success are exceedingly small. As I write about Hoylake I can see it all with a misty and sentimental eye. There are the white railings in front of the club; and Mr. Janion is standing in the porch in benignant contemplation, and Mr. Ball is wandering anon from the seventeenth green with his red-topped stockings, chipping the ball along with his iron as he goes; and I, knowing that somebody is going to beat me by seven up and six to play, yet long to be back there again.

Next in fame to Hoylake comes **Formby**, and there are many to be found who prefer it to the Cheshire course, though personally I do not consider their judgment a sound one. Formby is at any rate a most delightful course, and with that let us leave comparisons alone.

There is a particularly clear-cut distinction between the two parts of the course, which is in that respect a little like Sandwich. There is the country of the plains, on which the round begins and ends, and there is the country of hills wherein are all the middle holes. There is no doubt which are the prettier and more popular; the sand-hills would come out easily first in a general poll, but I have an uneasy sort of suspicion that the flat holes supply perhaps a better test of golf. There are, for instance, few better seventeenth holes than that which is to be found at Formby; just at the most crucial part of a hard-fought match it is as long and narrow and nerve-wracking as can be. Yet it is as flat as a pancake, and might from its appearance be a great many miles away from the sea. Still it is impossible to get over its intrinsic merits. There is the tee and there is the hole in an exact straight line, distant about two full shots away, and there is literally nothing in the way. That sounds terribly dull, but there would be nothing in the way if we drove down a Roman road, and yet it would be far from easy to keep on the course. To the right is a dreary tract of out-of-bounds, which is, to the morbid imagination, white with the countless balls that have been driven there. To the left is a narrow little ditch, and beyond the ditch rough and tussocky grass. To hit the tee-shot with reasonable accuracy ought not to be beyond our powers, but the second shot is undeniably a beast. We are undecided whether to aim out to the right and try for a hook or to the left for a slice, since for some reason it is horribly difficult to play a perfectly straightforward shot down a straightforward road of turf. We shuffle with our feet, become thoroughly uncomfortable, and—the precise form of disaster must be left to individual fancy.

The sixteenth, at which we traverse the same flattish country, is no bad hole either; nor are the first two or three, where we drive straight ahead, with plenty of cops and bunkers to keep us on the straight and narrow path. In old days there used to be an attractive tee-shot to the fourth hole over the corner of a group of trees, which seemed to be for ever heeling over under the force of the wind and mesmerically luring the slicer to his fate. That is changed now, however, and we go straight on to the old fifth green, and make our entry into the mountainous country rather earlier. Our first introduction to the hills comes at the old seventh, where there is a blind second shot into a big crater —a type of hole not now so favourably looked upon as it was once. Then comes a hole which we shall always remember, along an ominous gorge with frowning hills on either side of us. There is something romantic and mysterious about it, and if we retained the imagination of our childhood we should inevitably play at being an

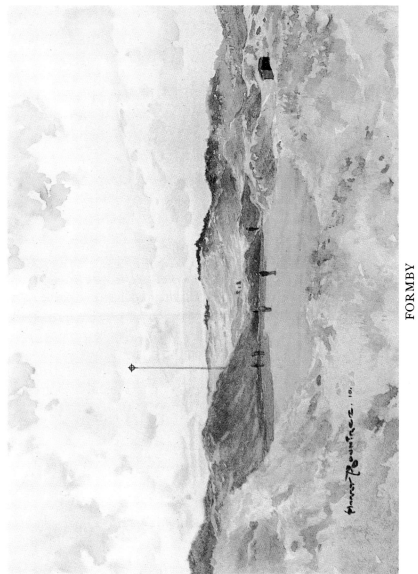

FORMBY

The old seventh green

invading army, with the enemy's sharp-shooters hidden in crevices among the hills.

After this comes the new country which has lately been taken in, and there are some fine two-shot holes—so fine that they will be three-shot holes for some of us—and some that are less strikingly excellent. We continue to dodge about among the great hills, roughly speaking, until we reach the fifteenth hole, but before that we shall have played another and particularly excellent hole along a narrow gully —the thirteenth. The last four holes lie on flatter country, although there is still every opportunity of getting into sand, and we finish with a good two-shot hole on to a fine big green in front of a fine big club-house. The greens are beautifully green; they are likewise very true and keen enough, without ever being bare and hard. The lies, too, are excellent, and it is altogether one of those courses where the player's fate is entirely in his own hands. If he plays well everything will conspire to help him on his way, but he has got to play really well—good, sterling, honest golf : there is no mistake about that at Formby.

Wallasey, where we come back to Cheshire again, is another course of mighty hills : indeed I do not think I have ever seen a course on which the contour of the hills and valleys was so infinitely picturesque. At several of the holes we play, or try to play, in the trough of two great waves of sand that tower on either side of us, and feel rather overpowered by the vastness of our surroundings. There was a time when Wallasey, though amusing enough, was too short and blind and tricky to be taken very seriously, but all that is changed now, and, with the addition of heaven knows how many hundreds of yards, the course is a long and punishing one. It is still perhaps a little too blind for those of very rigid and spartan views, but whatever the exact place which may be assigned to it on the day of judgment—and this sort of question will never be settled at any earlier date—it is undoubtedly good golf.

Certainly the first hole is the blindest of the blind. Wallop the first, and the ball vanishes over a hill; wallop the second—this time with a mashie—and it flies over another on to the green. This is not the best of beginnings, but the second has a much more interesting tee-shot, where we try to hug a bank covered with a particularly pestilent form of bush, and then at the third we are in the country of hills and valleys. The view at the third, as we look down the long winding gully that leads to the hole, is one of the most charming in golf; and the fifth is another wonderfully picturesque hole, with a terrifying second shot. After the seventh we leave the sandhills for a while, and play backwards and forwards for a spell along some flat holes that seem to radiate from one solitary house that stands alone in the middle of the course. They are very good holes some of them, and the ninth, eleventh, and thirteenth especially need long, straight hitting, but the last four or five holes take us back to the more characteristic country, and the finish comes in a blaze of glorious sandhills. A rather blind, and to the stranger a puzzling, tee-shot should land us safely on the table-land, and then far

WALLASEY
The fifth green

away and rather below us to the right we see the promised land, the seventeenth green, and with a good shot the ball will swoop away for an apparently incredible distance, and finish by the hole side. The eighteenth, too, is full of charm, and when we have successfully carried the spur of a big hill and played our second over some more bold and broken ground, we can hole out in a deep hollow, with the eyes of the whole club watching us from above as they sit in front of the club-house. It is quite likely that we have played very far from well, since this country of mountains and deep dells is always difficult for the stranger, and our host has probably ways and means of reaching the green that we are apt to regard as ways of darkness, but we shall have found the golf infinitely pleasant and exhilarating.

There are other Liverpool courses, Leasowe, Blundell-sands, Hesketh, Birkdale, and Southport, which are fully worthy of more extended notice, but we must be getting away from Liverpool to the links where the man from Manchester often plays his weekly golf—the course of the Lytham and St. Anne's Club. **St. Anne's** is not far from Blackpool, where there is incidentally quite a good course, and after the day's golf we can, if we have sufficient energy, go and dance in the largest dancing hall in the world or climb the highest tower in the world, or, in short, consult the advertisements of Blackpool. This, however, is not business, and we have to play serious golf at St. Anne's, for the opposition is very good and very keen, as the members of the Oxford and Cambridge Golfing Society have discovered to their cost.

As compared with Hoylake, St. Anne's is very smooth and trim, and just a little artificial. If the day is calm and we are hitting fairly straight, the golf seems rather easy than otherwise; and yet we must never allow ourselves to think so too pronouncedly, or we shall straightway find it becoming unpleasantly difficult. If there is a strong wind blowing we shall not even be tempted to think it easy, for there is plenty of rough grass on either side, and the hitting of a good straight tee-shot, which seemed so simple and made the holes seem simple, will be a cause of considerable anxiety. Whatever the weather and the wind, there is one thing that we ought always to do well at St. Anne's, and that is putt, for the greens are as good and true as any in the world, and can even challenge comparison with those in the Old Deer Park. Given an opponent who is a really fine putter—Mr. Lassen or some other inhuman fiend—and till he has played two more while our ball lies stone dead we can never feel quite happy; the truly-struck putt comes on and on over that wonderfully smooth turf and flops into the hole with a sickening little thud, and there are we left gasping and robbed of our prey. There is no kind of excuse for bad putting at St. Anne's, and in fine weather there is indeed little excuse for any form of error, for the lies are uniformly good and the stances uniformly smooth, save perhaps at two holes, where the land lies in ridges and furrows, and we may need a measure of skill to persuade the ball to fly from the hanging sides of a ridge.

124

LYTHAM AND ST. ANNE'S

The seventh tee

CHESHIRE AND LANCASHIRE

The trouble, besides rough grass and pot-bunkers, consists of sandhills, both natural and artificial. To build an artificial sandhill is not a light task, and it is characteristic of the whole-hearted enthusiasm of the golfers of St. Anne's that they have raised several of these terrifying monuments of industry. They are still in their infancy, and look just a little new and raw, but they will destroy the golfer's card and temper just as effectively as those that have stood from time immemorial. They are, moreover, covered with bent grass, which will no doubt increase and multiply to the greater glory of the hills and ruination of the golfer.

The course begins with a short hole of no particularly coruscating virtues, but the second and third are both good, and the railway on the right scares us into a hook : and the hook takes us into a bunker, and the bunker loses us the hole. The fourth has a very pretty green, well and naturally guarded by hummocks ; and Nature has been very kind again at the sixth, where there is a deep crater, to be comfortably reached in two good shots. Indeed these natural craters are rather a feature of the course, for there is something of the same kind to be found at the seventh, and a very perfect example at the fourteenth. The worst that is to be said against them is that they give some encouragement to a second shot off the back-wall, but the attendant risks are very great, and the back-wall shot that just misses the mark brings with it a peck of troubles.

The ninth has a fine tee-shot and a long, difficult, and blind second shot, in which the stranger always finds that he has aimed at the wrong chimney pot in a row of houses at Ansdell. The tenth has a hut for drinks and a tee-shot that fully justifies such an indulgence; while at the eleventh we must go on driving and driving till we reach the green, which, contrary to our expectations, we shall ultimately do. The thirteenth is of an unattractive and inlandish appearance, but is as good a hole as is to be found on the course, and needs the very straightest of play to avoid a network of bunkers. Out of a puddle in the bottom of one of these bunkers I once holed a pitch, and have never played the hole so well either before or since. Then comes the crater hole, the fourteenth before mentioned; and after that we may hope to get home with a three and three fours, but the four at the seventeenth is not a particularly easy one, and there is always a chance of too strong an approach being bunkered in a flower bed beyond the home green, to the great amusement of the spectators in the smoking-room window.

There is nowhere in the golfing world where keener opponents and more friendly hosts are to be found than in the counties of Lancashire and Cheshire, and I cannot help saying that I, along with my brothers of the Oxford and Cambridge Golfing Society, owe them a very deep debt of gratitude.

Before finally quitting Lancashire, we must look at one inland course, namely, **Trafford Park,** which may be accepted as the foremost among the purely Manchester courses. I was interested and surprised to find, in reading a little history of the Manchester Golf Club, that golf was played in Manchester at a date so utterly prehistoric as

TRAFFORD PARK

The club-house from the eighteenth tee

CHESHIRE AND LANCASHIRE

1818. However, a few enthusiasts really did play upon Kersal Moor at that remote period, and they called themselves the Manchester Golf Club. They had no imitators till sixty-four years later, when Mr. Macalister founded the Manchester St. Andrews Golf Club that played in Manley Park. The birth of this second club happened almost simultaneously with the death of the first. Kersal Moor, for all its solitary and savage name, fell a prey to the builder, and in 1883 the original Manchester Golf Club ceased to exist, and its name was assumed by the Manley Park Club. Since then, it should be added, it has, happily, come to life again under the title of the Old Manchester Golf Club.

Meanwhile, Manley Park came to share the fate of Kersal Moor, and a move was made to Trafford Park, which has now been the home of the Manchester Golf Club from 1893 to the present time. It has flourished ever since, and has played a prominent part in the golfing life of Manchester.

Trafford Park is a good course in spite of the most unpromising surroundings. All round the fine old park, formerly the home of the de Traffords, manufactories now raise their hideous heads, while along one side runs the Manchester Ship Canal, and the man who desires an excuse for a bad shot may allege that an ocean liner insisted on coming behind him just as he was playing. These are certainly not recommendations, but there are compensating advantages in good turf, good greens, good length holes, and the old mansion-house, which has been converted into one of the most comfortable and palatial of club-houses.

The turf is excellent. It is certainly not muddy, nor is it precisely sandy. One who has played much golf at Trafford describes it as 'peaty,' and I will leave it at that. The hazards are of the usual park description: trees, artificial bunkers, and at one hole a pond, while the ground is pleasantly undulating for the first nine holes, and rather too flat for the second.

We begin by driving downhill, which is always a comforting thing to do, although we ought to have warmed to our work a little in order to get full value out of a downhill drive. This takes us into the lower ground, and after a moderate first we have a really good two-shot hole for the second; well over four hundred yards long, and with a thoroughly interesting second shot on to a raised green. The third, which is a one-shot hole—there are four of these in all—takes us up a hill again, and of the holes that follow the fourth and the seventh are especially good, the former demanding a long, straight, iron shot on to a particularly well bunkered green.

Coming home the course suffers a little, as I said, from being too flat, and, so as with many of these park courses, it is rather hard to pick out any one hole from among its fellows. Good sound golf will be repaid, and so will the golf that is unsound and bad, but neither the rewards nor the punishments are of a thrilling or heroic order. There is one hole, however, that calls for special mention, the sixteenth, where two really fine shots are needed to reach the green, and the only thing to be said against the hole is that it would be better still if it were number seventeen instead; not that the present seventeenth is bad, but that the sixteenth is so eminently well adapted to occupy that critical and important position. Gaudin has been round the course in 65, but the intending visitor will be disappointed if he imagines that he himself will necessarily do a particularly low score on that account. In these days of expanded courses—against which one begins to see some signs of a revolt—Trafford Park is not vastly long, but it calls for good, honest golf for all that.

CHAPTER VII.

YORKSHIRE AND THE MIDLANDS.

WITH an open mind and a golfing friend I started in the month of March on a short pilgrimage to the courses of Yorkshire and the Midlands. Two rounds a day on a new course, to be followed by some hours of travelling, constitute a strenuous life for the ordinary golfer, although no doubt it is mere child's play to the great ' showmen ' of golf, as Mr. Croome has christened them. On my remarking on this point to my companion that we now knew what it must feel like to be Braid or Taylor, he replied that personally he did not feel in the very least like them, and that he did not think my play was any justification for my doing so either.

In spite of this slight unpleasantness, we had a most agreeable pilgrimage, which was begun by taking a train to Scarborough, in order to play at Ganton. **Ganton** sprang into fame as being the home course of Harry Vardon. It was there that he played the second half of his great match with Willy Park, and having gained a small but serviceable lead at North Berwick, played one of his most overpowering

GANTON

The carry at the eighteenth tee

games on his own course, and never gave his adversary even
the faintest of chances.   Some of the glamour of Harry
Vardon still hangs round Ganton, although he has left it now
for some years, and has a worthy successor in Edward Ray,
the hitter of mighty drives and smoker of many pipes.
The course has been a good deal altered since Vardon's
days, for with the advent of the Haskell, it suffered the
common lot and became rather too short.   Now it has been
stretched and rearranged and pretty severely bunkered;
most noteworthy of all, the hole of which the visitor to
Ganton formerly carried away the most vivid impression,
has been altered out of recognition.   This is the present
twelfth hole, where in old days the tee-shot consisted of a
mashie pitch, played mountains high into the air in order
to clear the tops of a row of tall trees.   Now the trees
have been ruthlessly cut down, and we have a one-shot
hole, demanding not a mashie but a brassey shot, very good
and very orthodox.   No doubt the old hole was a bad one,
and the new one is good; nevertheless there must have been
some bitter regrets over the felling of the trees.   Unless we
are utterly consumed with a fire of reforming zeal, we can
well afford to drop a tear over the disappearance of these
holes—once the pride and joy of their creators, now
destroyed or altered beyond recognition.   The once-
famous short holes are meeting with the same fate all over
the country.   The 'Maiden,' long since shorn of much of
its glory, is undergoing yet another metamorphosis, and it
is even rumoured that some day it will be a blind hole no
longer.   The 'Sandy Parlour' has even been threatened,

and indeed it may be laid down that if the golfers of a dozen years ago praised a hole as being 'sporting,' that hole will be the first marked down for the reformer's attack. It is all very splendid no doubt, but it is also just a little bit sad.

So much for the twelfth hole of blessed memory; and now we must get back to the course in general. To begin with, Ganton is a course of sand and fir trees and gorse bushes. It is a little like Woking, a little like Worplesdon; and, generally speaking, it is the type of course that one would expect to find in Surrey rather than in Yorkshire. Needless to say, however, it has plenty of character of its own, and in particular it possesses by far the vastest and generally most gorgeous bunker that is to be found, as far as I know, on any inland course. It is a huge pit of sand, with just the depths and shallows, the bays and promontories of the genuine seaside article. It is so large that, by its unaided efforts, it provides highly effective bunkering for the tee-shots to the two last holes; and as regards its dimensions, I shall not be flattering it very grossly if I compare it to the bunker in front of the fifth tee at Westward Ho! It is the more striking because it lies on the other side of a road away from the main body of the course; and after a series of trim little pot-bunkers, one comes quite suddenly upon it, rugged, natural, and magnificent.

Nature has done nearly all the bunkering work for these last two holes; at the others she has had to be assisted by man, and man has been very busy cutting pot-bunkers, and mostly towards the sides of the fairway and the edges of

132

the green. The bunkering seems to me, if I may say so, to be exceedingly well done, and for the most part one has to keep reasonably straight—sometimes very straight indeed—from the tee. The sixth, seventh, and eighth I remember particularly as all demanding scrupulously accurate tee shots, and of these perhaps the eighth is the most difficult, with serious bunkers on opposite sides of the course at just the distance of a moderately good drive; it is not unlike the tee-shot to the sixth at Woking, or the eighth at Walton Heath; and to say that is not to call the shot an easy one.

There are whins in fair profusion, and they play an important part at both the second and third holes. The approach to the second is a really difficult one, for the green lies in an angle made by two lines of whins, which are partially protected from the infuriated niblick player by formidable bunkers, so that any perceptible error is likely to bring with it a disaster either sandy or prickly. At the third, again—a very full one-shot hole—the whins guard the entire left-hand side of the course. It is, to be sure, possible to hit over them, but the feat entails a carry of some two hundred yards, and even Ray admits that a long shot is wanted to get clear to the left.

The criticism I feel disposed to make, very tentatively, of the first nine holes at Ganton is that they are a little too much of the same length. There is the third hole afore-mentioned, and there is the fifth, demanding an extremely pretty little pitch from the tee; nor must I forget the ninth, a really fine two-shot hole that winds its way along the

133

bottom of a little valley. At the other six one seems to be playing the second shot with the same straight-faced iron club. They are individually very good, but the least little bit in the world monotonous, and there is a more attractive variety about the home-coming nine.

Of these last nine nearly all are good; but the last three are, I think, the most attractive, being all interesting and all different. The sixteenth is a fine straight-hitting two-shot hole over undulating country. The seventeenth brings us face to face with the big bunker, and if the wind be favourable we may hope to reach the green with a really good hit, but the green is curly, tricky, and difficult of access. Finally, we have another drive over the big bunker for the last, taking care to avoid being stymied by a clump of firs, and then we may pitch comfortably home across the road with a four well in sight.

We had two rounds of Ganton on the first day of our pilgrimage—a warm, delightful, sunny day—and then took train to Huddersfield to play at Fixby. **Fixby** is as different from Ganton as chalk is from cheese, or as a watering-place is from a manufacturing town. Ganton is charmingly pretty in a way that is comparatively ordinary to anyone who has seen Surrey and Berkshire. Fixby has for the southerner's eye a kind of grim and murky romance. For some two miles we have to wend our way up a long slope through Huddersfield and its outskirts, looking rather drab and ugly and intensely prosperous. Then suddenly the romance begins. We climb up a steep hill through a pretty wood, albeit the trees are black with the smoke of many

134

HUDDERSFIELD

The club-house

chimneys, finally to emerge rather breathless in a new land. Now we are perched on the top of a hill, in wild, solitary, moorish country. A long way down below us are Huddersfield and its mills, and all around is a great stretch of view, rather bleak and sombre, but possessed of a very distinct beauty of its own. We are not really on the moors, but we feel as if we were, and all the colouring is moorland colouring. Everything is a subdued grey or green, and even the stone walls, which abound on the course, have a gloomy tint of their own—a kind of purplish black that I have never seen anywhere else. It strikes us at once that this course could only be in the north; there is nothing southern about it, and by this strangeness and strong character it casts something of a spell over the southern visitor. This is how I saw Fixby, with a grey leaden sky and a mighty wind blowing the misty rain that is called 'moor-grime' strongly in my face. In summer it must possess quite a different sort of beauty when the great clumps of rhododendrons are all in bloom, as the artist has depicted them, and the club-house in the centre of a blaze of gorgeous colour.

To turn from the scenery to the golf, there is a very clearly-marked distinction between the two rounds of nine holes, each of which begins and ends near Fixby Hall, which is used as the club-house. The first nine holes might be described as park golf; and yet this would be perhaps to give a false impression, for the trees do not play an important part, and the turf is harder and dryer than the normal park turf. It is plain-sailing, straightforward golf,

135

in which we can see where we are going, and the trouble
consists mainly of artificial bunkers of the ordinary type.

The second half is much more *sui generis*. We emerge
from the park land into country which is more open and
much more undulating. We have to play a great many
more blind shots—in fact, we have rather too many of
them; and there are one or two holes—exceedingly difficult
holes they are—which would be, I venture to think, much
better if only we could get a good view of the flag. Another
feature of the second half is the ubiquitous stone wall.
Sometimes it is an ordinary wall; sometimes it partakes of
the nature of a sunk fence, and we only realize its presence
by seeing our ball suddenly plunge, like another Curtius,
into the bowels of the earth. I should not like to pledge
myself as to the exact number of walls, but we shall be
lucky if we do not make acquaintance with more than one
of them upon a windy day; and, in parenthesis, the wind
can blow at Fixby with an energy worthy of the strongest
seaside gale. The two halves may fairly be summed up by
saying that the first half provides the sounder golf, and
the second the more exciting; and that both need a man
to play them.

On the way out the holes that I personally think the more
attractive are the fourth—a nice single shot, 170 yards
long, on to a plateau green—and a group of three that come
together, the sixth, seventh, and eighth. Of these the eighth
is a pretty enough little short hole with a very well-guarded
green, but the seventh is the best of the three and also the
most interesting, from the fact that it owes its merits almost

entirely to ingenuity in construction rather than to natural advantages.

The green has certainly a good natural protection to the right in the shape of a ditch, to which has been added a bunker on the left; but still, if we were allowed to make a direct frontal attack upon the hole, we should have no great difficulty to contend with. A frontal attack, however, has been forbidden us by Mr. Herbert Fowler's ingenuity. In the straight line between the tee and the green have been erected a series of formidable fortifications, wherefore we must drive out to the right and then approach the hole from the side. The further we go to the right the more difficult the approach will be, but if we can play with a judicious hook, and so ' pinch ' the fortifications as close as we dare, we shall obtain a reasonably open and easy approach. This device of compelling people to play the hole as a ' dog legged ' hole has made all the difference between a good and an ordinary hole. Of some of the longer holes on the way out I have said nothing, not because they are not sufficiently testing in character, but because they are for the most part straightforward holes that do not lend themselves to distinctive description.

After the turn comes, as I have said, the region of blind shots and stone walls. The twelfth is a curious hole, because of the extraordinary difficulty of judging the direction of the second shot over a high grassy mound. Even those who are steeped to the eyes in local knowledge are never quite certain if their ball will be lying close to the flag or thirty yards away, and race feverishly to the top of the mound to see what has befallen them. The thirteenth, again, has a puzzling, blind uphill approach, after a really good tee-shot across a wall. There is a good long, punishing finish, all the last three holes being over, and two of them well over, four hundred yards in length. At the last there is a chance, if the breeze be favourable, of a really fine second shot from the crest of a hill that shall send the ball soaring away for an apparently immeasurable distance, avoiding stone walls and trees, and ultimately reaching the green.

There is plenty of hard work to be done in reaching the greens at Fixby, and still more when we have reached them, for they are fast and curly to a degree, although very true when at their best, and there is much allowance to be made for borrow and much gentle trickling of the downhill putt. That Fixby is a difficult course is proved by the fact that the redoubtable Sandy Herd has never accomplished the full round of this his home course under 70. If 70 is Herd's best, anything under 80 is not to be despised by the ordinary mortal.

Continuing our journey of discovery in a southerly direction, we next took the train to Nottingham, and thence some few miles out to **Hollinwell**, passing on the way Bulwell Forest, formerly the home of the Notts Golf Club, but now converted into a very popular municipal course. Though Hollinwell is some miles out of Nottingham, the factory chimneys are not so far away, but that the ball, which starts its career on the first tee a snowy white soon passes through a series of varying greys till it is coal black, unless its

HOLLINWELL

Looking across the second green

complexion is renewed by the use of the sponge. The southern caddie's simple and natural method of cleaning a ball is not here to be recommended.

Hollinwell is a wonderfully sandy course, and when there is a strong wind one may see great clouds of sand blowing down the course after the most approved seaside fashion. The course is rather curiously shaped, since nearly all the holes lie in a long, wide valley. Sometimes we play down the valley, and sometimes we play across it, tacking this way and that, so that we are never hitting monotonously either with or against the wind. Sometimes also we scale the side of the valley and play along the top of the slope, and herein lies a certain weakness of the course, for these upland holes are not quite worthy of the rest. They are of the downland order, with blind shots, big perplexing slopes, and greens cut out of the sides of hills. Luckily there are but few of them, for they are but poor golf, whereas most of the holes in the valley are very good indeed.

I never saw a course that began with fairer promise, for the first hole looks and is delightful—a good long hole of well over 400 yards in length. To the right stretches a line of bracken, while on the left is a small clump of firs, just near enough to the line to induce a slice into the ferns. This first hole is so good that the other holes have a high standard to live up to, and in one important respect they perhaps do not quite succeed. That wilderness of bracken to the right holds out a promise which is not quite fulfilled, because that which Hollinwell lacks is rough ground severe

enough to punish the erratic driver. I have no doubt that
I was lucky, but I remember several of the most perfect lies
for a brassey which were meted out to me, when in common
justice I should have been plying my niblick. The rough's
bark is much worse than its bite, and one may often hit very
crooked and not be one penny the worse. More bunkers—
many more bunkers—at the sides of the course, and perhaps not quite so many in the middle would be no bad
prescription for Hollinwell.

If, however, the course has some faults, it also has many
merits, and the most attractive, because the most characteristic holes, are those in which the peculiar character
of the ground comes into play. Thus at both the seventh
and ninth we play across the breadth of the valley into little
gullies that run some way in between the spurs of the hill.
If we are perfectly straight, the gully receives us with open
arms, but to be at all seriously crooked is to be perched on
a hillside among thick grass and red sandstone. These are
both holes of a fine length, and though with hitting an
arrow-like straightness we may hope for fours, we need not
make undue lamentations over fives. The eleventh, again,
is a charming hole, where the way to the hole follows the
contour of a subsidiary valley that wanders away from the
main valley on some little expedition of its own; nor, to
retrace our steps, must the second be left out, with its pretty
background of trees and water.

After the eleventh the golf degenerates for a while, when
we leave the lowlands for the highlands; but, just as we are
feeling a little sad, comes a marked improvement at the

fifteenth, and we end with two really good holes, one short
and one long. To justify its existence as a seventeenth
hole, a short hole must needs be a very good short hole, and
this is an excellent one, save that the inordinately long
approach with the wooden putter should be prevented by a
bunker on the left. The eighteenth, except that it is a
good deal longer, is almost the converse of the first, and
the clump of firs that made us slice at the first tee will
certainly trap us if we pull our second shot. This last hole
lives in my memory from the fact that it gave to my companion a temporarily undeserved reputation among the
golfers of Nottingham. Having played a round of almost
unbroken sixes, he placed the ball close to the hole with a
long iron shot for his third, and holed the putt before an
awestruck assembly in the club-house window with an air
and manner suggesting that four was the highest rather than
the lowest score that he had accomplished during the round.
What is more, he only just failed to do the same thing in
the afternoon, although the hole is 555 yards long. Such
is the inveterate habit that some people have of playing to
the gallery.

From Nottingham our way lay to Birmingham, where we
were to play at **Sandwell Park**. A train journey to a
melancholy and mysterious place called Spon Lane, followed
by "a penny to the left and a penny to the right" (as we
were advised) in a tramcar brought us to West Bromwich.
West Bromwich is a name calculated to thrill the football
devotee with glorious memories of West Bromwich Albion,
but it is not in itself a particularly attractive spot. Yet

GOLF COURSES

Sandwell Park must once have been a beautiful place before the houses began to crowd round its gates and the colliery chimneys to pour black volumes of smoke across it. It is a fine park still, if one can only blind oneself to the houses and the chimneys; but that, save in one or two secluded corners, is a difficult task—Birmingham is too all-pervading to permit of many illusions.

We did not see Sandwell under very favourable conditions as regards weather. There was every now and again a flurry of snow, and a most piercingly cold wind blew across the course, rendering useless any number of waistcoats and mittens, and robbing the fingers of all power of gripping the club. It is very difficult under such circumstances to judge of the length of any particular hole, for the wind laughs at yard measures, and reduces a good length hole to a drive and a pitch, and converts a drive and a pitch into a three-shot hole.

Perhaps it was the effect of first going out to face the icy blast, but I thought the first few holes at Sandwell rather poor, being of a hybrid length and not particularly exciting. The golf improves wonderfully, however, as it goes on, and from the seventh onward is infinitely more interesting. The eighth needs a very straight drive, followed by a very delicate second shot—a tricky shot in whatever way we start to play it. If we pitch up the hill, we must pitch just up and no further; while if we run the shot, the hill is just steep enough to induce a lively fear that the ball will refuse to climb it. Moreover, when I played it, the hole was cut with fiendish cunning very close to the top of the hill, so

SANDWELL PARK

Mr. Woolley driving from the 'Pulpit' tee

that the very nicest judgment was necessary in order to avoid a long, sloping and curly putt. The ninth consists of an absolutely blind pitch with a small crater, reminding one of a very old but not very highly esteemed friend, the 'Crater' hole at Aberdovey. Then comes a hole that is really good, and it seemed to me the best on the course— two honest shots along a narrow neck of turf, which tapers perceptibly as it nears the green.

By this time we have reached the highest point of the links, and now descend into the lowlands again, driving from the 'Pulpit' tee to a green which lies in front of the big, white, gloomy house, whence the owner has long since retired, smoked out by the colliery chimneys. A good two-shot hole follows, and next comes one of the most amusing of short holes, which, whether intrinsically good or bad, deserves to escape the zeal of the inconoclast because of its singular character. One hundred and thirty are all the yards it can boast, but between tee and green a terrible monster rears its head in the form of some ancient rifle butts. They tower so high above and so close to us that even with a mashie and a teed ball we are all too likely to err. Moreover, it is not merely a matter of getting over at any price. The hole is quite close to the butts on the far side, and only the ball that shall just drop over and no more should satisfy us. Circumstances alter cases, of course, and with his opponent having the honour and failing to get over, a man may well play his shot with a brassey if he have a mind to it. Then, indeed, it is a case of over at any price, for the ground short of the butts is terribly rough, and a brilliant recovery is not in the least probable. It is the hole that must have been the grave of many hopes, perhaps even of some foursome friendships; and yet, if we were out practising with half a dozen old balls and no one to look at us, we could do as many twos and threes as ever we wanted.

There are some other good holes to follow, but they appear comparatively orthodox and ordinary after that quaint little thirteenth. One of the best things about the course is the turf, which is very springy and pleasant to walk upon. This old park turf very often proves sadly disappointing when it comes to making putting greens out of it, but the Sandwell greens are excellent, and in more propitious weather must be delightful to putt upon.

Not far from Sandwell Park is another very well-known Birmingham course, **Handsworth**. This is the home green of that keenest and most persevering of golfers, Mr. C. A. Palmer; he has tried as hard over his own course as he did over his own game, and the system of bunkers, for which he has chiefly been responsible, is marked by a great deal of skill and ingenuity. The course is undoubtedly a good sound test of golf, and there is one type of golfer who will be tested out of his seven senses, and that is the victim of a chronic slice. All along the right-hand side of the course there runs an out-of-bounds area, so that the poor slicer is for ever dropping another ball over his shoulder.

Another hazard that plays an important part, especially in those holes that come in the middle of the round, is a

HANDSWORTH

The first tee

stream. Full and ingenious use has been made of this stream, and there is a good deal of rather cunning pitching to be done in order to circumvent it; anything in the nature of a running shot is, naturally enough, at a discount.

The course begins quite excellently, and the first two holes are two of the best on the way out. At the first there is a big pool on the right and a generous supply of bunkers on the left, so that the very first tee-shot of the day has to be hit quite unpleasantly straight. If it is so hit, an iron shot of moderate length should see us safely on the green with the orthodox two putts for a four; if it is not, it would be rash to dogmatize as to what our precise score may be. The second hole, again, has one of those interesting carries from the tee that the player can make just as short or as long as he likes, according as his tactics are those of Fabius or some more dashing hero. The green lies on a hill-top some 380 yards away from the tee, and a bold tee-shot, followed by a really well-struck second, may make a four hole of it, but it is a good four.

The sixth is another good hole, although there is rather an aggravating cart track at just such a distance from the tee as to be likely to trap a respectable shot. The green, moreover, is very well guarded by a brook on the left and some pot-bunkers on the right. At the eighth we come to the first of the regular short holes, of which there are three in all, though there are two more which may on occasion be reached with a particularly shrewd blow, and it may be said in parenthesis that it is something of a weakness in the course that none of the three can be called passionately interesting.

It is to be hoped that we get a three at this eighth, for we shall need a little cheering before facing the prospect of real, honest hitting at the next three holes. The ninth is well over four hundred yards long, and we begin the homeward round with a five-hundred-yarder, or something very little short of it. It is not a very thrilling hole, however, and the fourteenth and seventeenth, both good two-shot holes, are certainly more interesting, and perhaps the best in the homeward nine.

The whole course is in good order, and the greens thoroughly well kept, although they are perhaps rather lacking in variety and err on the side of flatness. The soil is good and light, and that is no small thing to be thankful for in the very centre of England, when the nearest seaside golf is as far off as the coast of Wales.

CHAPTER VIII.

OXFORD AND CAMBRIDGE.

THE Universities of Oxford and Cambridge are rich in many things, but are very decidedly poor in the matter of golf courses. I should be more precise if I said poor in their own courses, for in Frilford Heath and Worlington (or as it is often called, Mildenhall) they are lucky to possess hospitable neighbours, who provide them with very delightful golf indeed.

The courses of Cambridge I know very well indeed, having played over them at intervals during the greater part of my life. With those of Oxford I have only, comparatively speaking, a bowing acquaintance, founded on the annual match between the University and the Oxford and Cambridge Golfing Society. Before turning to Frilford there is a word to be said of Cowley, Radley, and Hinksey, the latter of which has now ceased to exist. Cowley, so I have heard my friend Mr. Croome declare, is now rather a good course, and as I have never seen it, I most certainly will not venture to contradict him; but I can take my oath as to both Hinksey and Radley that they call for some other

147

epithet. **Hinksey** was certainly amusing, and I have spent some not wholly unpleasant afternoons there squelching through the mud and trying vainly to hole putts by cannoning off alternate wormcasts. There was a short hole—the fourth, I think—where one played a pitching shot into the heart of a wood which was distinctly entertaining, but on the whole it was not a good test of golf, or, if it was, then I would rather have my golf tested in some other way.

When Hinksey ceased to exist **Radley** came into being, and it is most decidedly a longer and more difficult course, but I am not certain that it is such good fun. It is a good deal longer; indeed a great many of the holes are of a very good length. There is a really good seventeenth, where one skirts a wood on the right, and granted a good lie—a thing which rests upon the knees of the gods—one may hit two really fine shots and get a fine four. I imagine, however, that no one will be prepared to deny that it is muddy—I will go so far as to say extremely muddy—and in these days we are so pampered with beautiful sandy inland courses that we no longer suffer mud at all gladly. So if we are at Oxford I think we had better throw economy to the winds and charter a 'taxi,' which shall take us up Cumnor Hill to Frilford Heath.

Frilford is only seven miles from Oxford, but it might be a hundred miles from anywhere. It lies on a little unfrequented by-road, and is as utterly rural and peaceful a spot as could be found anywhere. Here is sand enough and to spare—a wonderful oasis in the desert of mud. The sand is so near the turf that out of pure exuberance it

FRILFORD HEATH

Approaching the ninth green

breaks out here and there in little eruptions on the surface or flies up in a miniature sand-storm as the ball alights. The ground is for the most part very flat, and there are fir trees and whins scattered here and there. There is also a pretty wood of firs and birches, over which we have to drive at the third hole, of which more anon. The greens are a little rough as yet, and some of the bunkers have still to be made, or at least had not been made when I last played there; but time alone is wanted to make Frilford a very fine course indeed. It is already a wonderfully charming one.

The first two holes remind one a little of Muirfield, since there is a stone wall over which a pulled ball will inevitably vanish. The second is a fine long two-shot hole, and at the first, which is somewhat shorter, a highly ingenious use has been made of a solitary tree, which forces the player to drive close to the stone wall if he is to have an open approach. Then comes the third before mentioned, which is a one-shot hole. The wood rises pretty steeply in front of the tee, and the shot is made the more difficult because a cleek is hardly long enough, and so we have to take a wooden club. Many a shot that would under ordinary circumstances fill us with a mild degree of conceit will only send the ball crashing into the forest. It is no hole for the ' low raker ' which we regard with complacency at Hoylake and St. Andrews. We must hit a fine high towering shot, and then we may hope to find our ball on the green—a pretty little green which nestles close under the lee of the wood on the far side. After this come some long open holes

149

in a country of scattered whin bushes. Exactly how long they are I am not prepared to say. I played them in the company of Mr. A. J. Evans, and he appeared to regard them justifiably enough as two-shot holes, but personally I found myself taking by no means the most lofted of my iron clubs for my third shot. There is a pretty little pitching hole over a stone wall—the seventh—which has a flavour of Harlech about it; and the ninth, which brings us close to the club-house again, is surely one of the most alarming holes in existence. The drive is simple enough, but my goodness, what a second! In front of the green is a mountain, and on either side of the green are deep pits, towards which the ground 'draws' most unmistakably. Then the green itself is quite small, and has in its centre a copy of the aforesaid mountain in miniature. The approach shot, moreover, is by no means a short one, but is for the ordinary driver a good firm iron shot, so that a four is really an epoch-making score for the hole.

After the turn it seems to me that the golf shows a distinct falling off. The holes are still long enough and difficult enough, and Mr. Evans still seemed to require one stroke less to reach the green than I did, but for the most part they lack the indefinable charm of the first nine. There is, however, certainly one exception to this general criticism, and that is the really fascinating seventeenth, which is emphatically the right hole in the right place. There is a wood and a stone wall to carry, and the angle at which we play is such that there is a very real reward for the long ball which is judiciously hooked. A good as opposed to an ordinary drive may make all the difference between a four and a five, for the green is full of undulations, and the nearer we are to it when we take our iron in hand the better. Taking it altogether the golf is both good and difficult, and besides that Frilford is essentially one of those places where it is good to be alive with a golf club in one's hand—even if one uses it indifferently—and whither one looks forward to returning with a very keen enjoyment.

The undergraduates of Cambridge, when they have not the time to go to Worlington, now play golf at Coton, a pleasant little village enough that lies off the Madingley Road. I must spare a word or two, however, for the old course at **Coldham Common**, because I am quite sure that it was the worst course I have ever seen, and many others would probably award it a like distinction. The way to Coldham was suggestive of the pleasures that awaited one there, for it led down that most depressing of Cambridge streets, the Newmarket Road, and through the most unattractive slums of Barnwell. After voyaging for some distance along the Newmarket Road, one turned down a particularly black and odorous lane, crossed a railway bridge, and reached a flat, muddy expanse of grass, of which the only features were a railway line and some rifle butts. I should also perhaps include among its features a particularly pungent smell, which we always believed—I know not with how much truth—to proceed from the boiling down of deceased horses into glue.

On arriving outside the precincts of the club-house one was at once surrounded and nearly swept from one's legs

GOLF COURSES

by a yelling mob of caddies of most villainous appearance, who were supposed, quite erroneously, to be under the control of a well-meaning but deservedly superannuated policeman. Anyone who played there regularly soon found himself made over, body and soul, to one of these ruffians, and then exchanged the solicitations of the general mob for the unceasing importunities of his own particular henchman in the matter of cast-off clothing.

In addition to the regular corps of caddies there was an irregular body of younger depredators who had no official position, and earned a precarious livelihood by stealing or retrieving balls. They enjoyed considerable opportunities, because there were on the Common a good many muddy ditches—the only natural hazards—and along the edges of these ditches the youth of Barnwell took up strategic positions at stated intervals. Sometimes considerations of policy dictated that they should retrieve the errant ball, and return it to its owner for a penny. Sometimes they would dexterously stamp the ball into the mud, pretend to hunt for it with a great show of energy, and pocket it at their leisure when the owner had abandoned the search. This was an easy matter enough, for the mud was of the softest and thickest, and the ball would frequently bury itself on alighting without any help from the human foot. How our visitors from Blackheath and Yarmouth could bear it I now find a difficulty in understanding, and it says much for their enthusiasm and friendliness that they came to play against us year after year. They put up with it manfully, and very jolly matches we used to have. Indeed, to quote

152

OXFORD AND CAMBRIDGE

J. K. S., "the smile on my face is a mask for tears," and I could almost wish to strike another ball at Coldham. I must admit to having enjoyed myself very much there, almost as much as on another course of woeful greens and superlative muddiness—the old Athens course at Eton.

Coton I do not know well, but though an enthusiastic captain of Cambridge once told me that the greens were as good as the best seaside ones, I am disposed to think he was romancing. There is another flourishing course on the Gog-Magog hills, where there is at least a charming view, and twelve or thirteen miles away is Royston. Here there is a truly splendid view over miles and miles of the flat country, for the course lies on a piece of breezy downland perched high above its surroundings. A very jolly place it is whereon to play golf, though the golf perhaps is not of the highest class. It is a course of steep hills and deep gullies, and there is much climbing to be done and much putting on perplexing slopes. Some of these gullies form wonderful natural amphitheatres, and I always like to think that in one of them was fought the battle for the championship of England between Peter Crawley, the 'Young Rump Steak,' and Jem Ward, 'the Black Diamond.' That the fight took place on Royston Heath we know from *Boxiana*, but the exact battlefield has become obscured by the mists of time.

Better than all these courses, however, is **Worlington**, the home of the Royal Worlington and Newmarket Golf Club, who kindly allow the University to use their course and play their matches there. To get from Cambridge to

153

GOLF COURSES

Worlington is rather a serious undertaking, for although the station, Mildenhall, is but a little over twenty miles away, the progress made by the infrequent trains is of the most leisurely. Still, we do get there in time, passing poor deserted Coldham Common on the way, and the golf is good enough to repay us for all our trouble. Worlington is not unlike Frilford in appearance, being extremely solitary, flat, and sandy, and dotted here and there with fir trees. There are only nine holes, but of these several are really excellent, and none can fairly be said to be dull. One curious feature of the course is that one may play a round there which shall be made up almost entirely of fives and threes. This was conspicuously the case in the days of the gutty ball, for there were four holes that could be reached from the tee, although the second hole certainly required a very long shot, and five which were beyond the range of two full shots, save for colossal drivers. Whoever laid out the course clearly had no great opinion of Mr. Hutchinson's doctrine as to the length of a hole being some multiple of a full drive, and had no objection to two drives and a pitch. Nowadays with the rubber ball some of the old-time fives have become fours, but they are difficult fours requiring in one or two cases fine long-carrying second shots, and fives are still likely to preponderate.

Of all the courses that I know well, none shows so well as Worlington the difference between the solid and the elastic ball, and a particular instance, which is historic in a very small way, may be given. The third hole is an extraordinarily good one, wherein the green lies just

154

MILDENHALL

The result of a bad slice at the sixth

beyond a marshy ditch and is also well protected by pot-bunkers. After the tee-shot, one has to carry ditch, bunkers and all, but a weak drive necessitates playing short, and the shot is an extremely difficult one, because the ball has to be placed on a narrow neck of grass which slopes down on either side to a ditch and other horrors. Just before I went up to Cambridge there had been a great foursome between Douglas Rolland, Willy Park, Hugh Kirkaldy, and Jack White, who was then the professional at Worlington; and a certain shot of Rolland's was spoken of with bated breath as being something altogether super-human. With a fair breeze against him, he had actually reached the third green with his second shot. The hole is still the same length : the tee is back as far as it will possibly go, and yet one can as a rule get home with an iron club of no inordinate power, while it takes a very strong wind indeed to make it necessary to play short. This third is a wonderfully good hole still, but it was more heroic in the old days.

A hole that does to-day require two heroic shots is the sixth; indeed the green can only be reached in two with a favouring wind. Along the whole length of the hole, on the right-hand side, runs a belt of fir trees, while in front of the green is a ditch. If one clings very closely to the firs with the tee-shot, and then plays a big, high-carrying brassey shot, one may hope to see the ball just clear the last fir tree and drop down close to the hole. Another hole that nobody is ever likely to forget is the fifth. One may reach the green with a pitch from the tee, but what a difficult pitch it is. The green is something in the shape of a hog's back; immediately on the left of it is a stagnant pool of water, and on the right is a stream, complicated by overhanging willows. To reach the green is one distinct feat; to hole out in two putts, when one has got there, is another. For the most part the whole course is delightfully dry and sandy, in spite of the presence of many ditches, and the greens, when they are good, are very good, though they have sometimes a tendency towards getting a little bare and tricky.

It is no small thing for the Cambridge teams to have this admirable practising ground, and this alone should make for an improvement in Cambridge golf. University golf, however, has naturally improved a good deal in the last few years. Twelve years ago a freshman who should come up to either University and show himself to be already a good or even a goodish golfer was something of a phenomena. Nowadays thousands of school boys play golf, and consequently there is nearly always a supply of freshmen who can play a good game when they first come up. In the last century—to use a formidable expression—there was usually a considerable gap between the first two or three men and the last. In the very earliest days Oxford had two very fine players in Mr. Horace Hutchinson and Mr. Alexander Stuart, while Cambridge had Mr. Welsh, now a tutor at Jesus, and the possessor of a monumental reputation at Machrihanish. The other members of the side were generally of a very different calibre, and some of them would be badly off nowadays with any handicap under

156

eighteen. Later on in the early nineties Cambridge had some fine sides, with Mr. Low, Mr. Colt, Mr. Eric Hambro, and other good players, and to this day probably the best University side that ever played was the much quoted Oxford side of 1900, of which Mr. Mansfield Hunter was the captain.

On the whole, however, the general standard of play is higher to-day, and personally I was enormously struck with the golf in the match at Hoylake in 1910. For one thing, the driving was wonderfully steady and good, and some of it very long, and all the play was well worth the watching, which is more than could have been said for some of it not so very, very long ago.

CHAPTER IX.

A LONDON COURSE.

BY A LONG HANDICAP MAN.

I SHOULD like at the outset briefly to explain who I am and why I am writing this chapter. I am known to every golfer—I play fairly regularly, generally on a Saturday afternoon, sometimes in the evening during the summer; I am genuinely keen on the game, and can honestly say that I devote a good deal of thought and attention to it; I enter for all the competitions at my club, but my name rarely appears on the list of those who have returned scores —my card is generally torn up about the fourteenth hole, frequently earlier. I believe that I come in for a good deal of abuse at the hands of the very low handicap man. "These chaps ought not to be allowed on the course," or "There should be a special time for starting these long handicap men," or again, "My good sir, I've seen the man in front of me play his third, and he's not yet reached the bunker yet!" These and similar remarks are samples of what one has to bear.

A LONDON COURSE

One might perhaps gently remind the impatient expert that, after all, we long handicap men do serve some useful purpose; they, too, were once even as we are now, and, moreover, without us the spoils of the fortnightly 'sweep' would be distinctly lessened; now and again, also, one of us suddenly 'comes on his game,' and, if it be in a knock-out competition, spreads havoc and devastation among the players with handicaps of under six.

I am sometimes inclined to think that the long handicap player gets quite as much, if not more, enjoyment from his golf than does the man who receives only a small number of strokes from scratch. We are not so much depressed when we miss our drive, because it happens to us so much more frequently, and the joy we experience when we execute a perfect shot (and this *does* sometimes happen) is all the keener because of its comparative rarity. Furthermore, our anguish, when we are 'right off our game,' can be nothing in comparison with that of the skilled golfer who is in a similar condition (and I understand that this happens to even the greatest—have we not heard of Vardon failing at two-foot putts and Massy missing the ball altogether?)

I have been privileged to read Mr. Darwin's account of the famous courses of the British Isles, and it has been suggested that the thought might occur to long handicap players like myself that, reading of these fours and threes which figure so frequently, one may be tempted to despair and say, " This is all very fine for the plus man, but what sort of a game could I play on such a course? *My* low,

159

raking shot will not land me home on to the green; it will, I know, inevitably take me into a bunker—in how many strokes may I reasonably expect to accomplish the hole?"

I propose, therefore, under the kindly veil of anonymity, to describe the course on which I habitually play, from my point of view; the scratch man may skip this chapter or glance at it with amused scorn; it may possibly be of interest to my long-handicap fellows, who will, at anyrate, sympathize with my appreciation of dangers and terrors unsuspected by the more expert player.

The course is, like so many links in the neighbourhood of London, essentially a summer course; in the winter it is little better than a mud heap; we have a local rule which allows us (from October to March) to lift and drop without penalty if the ball is buried—and in the ordinary friendly match the wiser players agree to tee their balls through the green rather than laboriously hack them out of the villainous lies, where they are almost inevitably to be found during the winter months.

But in summer it can hold its own with most inland courses; the situation is delightful, the views extensive, and one can scarcely believe that one is not far from the four-mile radius.

The course is crowded on a fine Saturday afternoon, and it is necessary to put down a ball and give our names to a starter. We note that the man who put down a ball just after us whispers to his opponent: we also know quite well what he is saying, though we cannot hear him. "It will be all right, they are sure to lose a ball at the first two or

three holes,"—to which the other replies under his breath,
" No such luck, they don't hit far enough to lose a ball ! "

Our first drive is of the type described by Mr. Darwin
as ' exhilarating '—that is, we stand on a height and drive
down a hill. The plus men take their cleeks (when the
wind is behind them), and wait until the party in front is off
the green; we do not take a cleek, but we wait, from pride
of heart rather than fear of manslaughter, until the starter
says, " All right now, sir ! "

After our stroke we say, " It's brutal driving off before
a gallery ! " After his, he replies, " Yes, it always puts
me off."

There are several other holes of an ' exhilarating '
character—the eighth, fourteenth and fifteenth—at the
first-named there is splendid opportunity of driving out of
bounds; at the fourteenth we should strongly advise the
player to avoid the wire-netting about twenty yards in front
of the tee to the left; the stance for the second shot leaves
a good deal to be desired. A really fine slice at the
fifteenth will take us comfortably on to the green—but it is
the fourteenth green, and, choose we never so wisely the
spot on which to drop our ball, there still remains a hedge
to negotiate : it is not an easy green to approach—if you
elect to play short of the green and run on, your ball stops
dead; while if you play a nice, firm shot on to the green, it
invariably abandons all idea of being a pitch at all, and
suddenly converts itself into a magnificent running approach and careers gaily right across the green towards
the ninth flag.

GOLF COURSES

The third is our short hole; a good, honest thump with a mashie lands us in the hedge on the left of the green, whence recovery is somewhat difficult, while the ordinary foozle meets with an even worse fate in a hedge just in front; in the ditch beyond the first hedge is a large heap of cut grass. There is ample opportunity here for skilful niblick work, which compels the admiration of the two or three couples behind us, who have meanwhile collected on the tee.

The ninth is a shortish hole, for which one is popularly supposed to take an iron club. As this course of action always results in our having to play a long second out of the rough, we usually take a wooden club and slice into the tennis courts or the field beyond. With our third we may reach a cross-bunker, and a well-executed niblick shot takes us into a ditch on the other side. We wend our way once more behind the bunker (fortunately, we cannot hear the remarks of the couple behind us), and with a skimming, half-topped mashie shot reach the edge of the green. Three firm putts should see us down, winning the hole from our adversary, who misses a 'very short one.'

The sixteenth is the long hole; it has, I believe, been done in four; it has also been done in fourteen—I can vouch for the latter figure. There is nothing very terrible about the drive : one may certainly go unpleasantly near a tree and a hedge, but only a very long driver, slicing his best, can hope to reach them; it is true, a bad pull lands us in a ditch which runs parallel to the fairway, but the usual topped ball merely comes to rest in very moderately rough

162

grass. Our second shot needs some 'placing,' for the path which runs through the bunker is perilously narrow—we shall probably do better to play short deliberately (in which case I always find that I can hit so much farther than I had supposed); little by little, we make our way up the slope to the ditch in front of the fourteenth tee, and from there you may take any number of strokes to the green, according as you avoid the very long grass.

Perhaps the best hole on the course is the thirteenth. A sliced drive disturbs the equanimity of players coming to the seventeenth green, but a long second takes us out of danger of sudden death, and lands us comfortably in a cross-bunker. If, in addition to our crime of topping, we have added that of slicing, we have brought ourselves well up against some very awkward trees, and, in extricating ourselves from these, anything may happen. If we escape double figures here, we may consider that we are at the top of our form.

It is of no use to hope that your drive will jump the bunker at the fifth : I have tried the long, low, raking shot here many times, but the bunker is too high and too far away to be run through successfully; it is much better to slice unblushingly into comparative safety. Our second shot needs to be spared—my 'spared' shots usually travel about ten yards—but a 'low, scuffling' shot runs obligingly down the slope, and may (or may not) stop on the green. Another way, as Mrs. Glasse says, is to play violently to the left, strike the bank and run down towards the hole—it is necessary, however, to carry out the second part of the programme, or we may be in serious trouble in the rough.

At the end of our round we return to the club-house, flushed with healthy exercise, with a full and particular knowledge of the bunkers of the course, but with the proud consciousness that we have not been passed, and that we have faithfully replaced every divot.

CHAPTER X.

ST. ANDREWS, FIFE AND FORFARSHIRE.

REALLY to know the links of St. Andrews can never be
given to the casual visitor. It is not perhaps necessary
to be one of those old gentlemen who tell us at all too
frequent intervals that golf was golf in their young days,
that we of to-day are solely occupied in the pursuit of pots
and pans, and that Sir Robert Hay, with his tall hat and
his graduated series of spoons, would have beaten us, one
and all, into the middle of the ensuing week. Such a
degree of senile decay is fortunately not essential, but one
ought to have known and loved and played over the links
for a long while; and I can lay no claims to such knowledge as that. I can speak only as an occasional pilgrim,
whose pilgrimages, though always reverent, have been far
too few. I do not know by instinct whether or not my
ball is trapped in 'Sutherland'; I only just know the difference between 'Strath' and the 'Shelly' bunker; I could
not keep up my end in an argument as to the proper line to
take at the second hole—I am, in short, a very ignorant
person, who means thoroughly well.

GOLF COURSES

There are those who do not like the golf at **St. Andrews,**
and they will no doubt deny any charm to the links themselves, but there must surely be none who will deny a charm
to the place as a whole. It may be immoral, but it is
delightful to see a whole town given up to golf; to see the
butcher and the baker and the candlestick maker shoulder-
ing his clubs as soon as his day's work is done and making
a dash for the links. There he and his fellows will very
possibly get in our way, or we shall get in theirs; we shall
often curse the crowd, and wish whole-heartedly that golf
was less popular in St. Andrews. Nevertheless it is that
utter self-abandonment to golf that gives the place its
attractiveness. What a pleasant spectacle is that home
green, fenced in on two sides by a railing, upon which lean
various critical observers; and there is the club-house on
one side, and the club-maker's shop and the hotels on the
other, all full of people who are looking at the putting, and
all talking of putts that they themselves holed or missed on
that or on some other green. I once met, staying in a
hotel at St. Andrews, a gentleman who did not play golf.
That is in itself remarkable, but more wonderful still, he
joined so rationally, if unobtrusively, in the perpetual
golfing conversation that his black secret was never discovered. I do not know if he enjoyed himself, but his
achievement was at least a notable one.

I am writing this chapter, when I am but newly returned
from St. Andrews, after having watched all the champions
of the earth play round the course for three strenuous days.
The weather was perfect; there was scarcely a breath of

166

ST. ANDREWS

The town in the distance

ST. ANDREWS, FIFE, FORFARSHIRE

wind, and violent storms of rain had reduced the glassy greens to a nice easy pace.   Scores of under eighty were absurdly plentiful, and, indeed, if someone had come in with a score of under seventy I think the news would have been received without any vast degree of astonishment. Yet, with all this brilliant, record-breaking golf being played over it, the course never looked really easy.   The champions certainly got their fours in abundance, but they had to work reasonably hard for most of them.   Nor did one suffer from the delusion, as one does when playing the part of a spectator upon simple courses, that one could háve done just as many fours oneself.   St. Andrews never looks really easy, and never is really easy, for the reason that the bunkers are for the most part so close to the greens. It is possible, of course, to play an approach shot straight on the bee line to the flag, and if we play it to absolute perfection all may go' well; but let it only be crooked by so much as a yard, or let the ball, as it often will do, get an unkind kick, and the bunker will infallibly be our portion. Consequently the prudent man will agree with Willy Smith of Mexico, who declared that it was unwise to " tease the bunkers "; he will not attempt to avoid these greedy, lurking enemies by inches or even feet, but he will give them a good wide berth and avoid them by yards.   The result of this policy is that the man who is getting his string of fours has to be continually laying the ball dead with his putter from a reasonably long way off, and so St. Andrews is a fine course for him who can do good work at long range with a wooden putter.

GOLF COURSES

Let not the reader hastily assume that his only difficulty at St. Andrews will be to keep out of the clutches of the bunkers lying close to the greens; he will find plently more stumbling-blocks in his path. There is the matter of length, for instance. The holes, either out or home, do not look very long when Braid is playing them with the wind behind him, but it is an entirely different matter when we have to play them ourselves with the wind in our teeth. Then we shall very often be taking our brasseys through the green, and yet be doing tolerably well if we have nothing higher than a five. There are a great many holes that demand two good shots, as struck by the ordinary mortal; there are three that he cannot reach except with his third, and there are only two that he can reach from the tee, of which one by common consent is the most fiendish short hole in existence. Thus we have two difficulties, that the holes are long, and that there are bunkers close to the greens; now, for a third, those greens are for the most part on beautiful pieces of golfing ground, which by their natural conformation, by their banks and braes and slopes, guard the holes very effectively, even without the aid of the numerous bunkers.

Providence has been very kind in dowering St. Andrews with plateau greens, and they are never easy to approach. A plateau usually demands of the golfer that a shot should be played; it will not allow him merely to toss his ball into the air with a lofting iron and the modest ambition that it may come down somewhere on the green. Again, a plateau never gives any undeserved help to the inaccurate approacher, as do the greens that lie in holes and hollows. Even in a more marked degree than at Hoylake, the ground is never helping us; in its kindest mood it is no more than strictly impartial. Finally, the turf is very hard, and consequently the greens are apt to take on a keenness that is paralyzing in its intensity.

Having by alarming generalizations induced in the unfortunate stranger a suitably humble frame of mind, the time has now arrived to take him over the course in some detail. The first thing to point out to him is the historic fact that there were once upon a time but nine holes, and that the outgoing and incoming players aimed at the self-same hole upon the self-same green. That state of things has necessarily long passed away, but the result is still to be seen in the fact that most of the greens are actually or in effect double greens, and consequently the two processions of golfers outward and inward bound pass close to each other, not without some risk to life and much shouting of ' Fore ! '

With this preliminary observation, we may tee up our ball in front of the Royal and Ancient Club-house for one of the least alarming tee-shots in existence. In front of us stretches a vast flat plain, and unless we slice the ball outrageously on to the sea beach, no harm can befall us. At the same time we had much better hit a good shot, because the Swilcan burn guards the green, and we want to carry it and get a four. It is an inglorious little stream enough : we could easily jump over it were we not afraid of looking foolish if we fell in, and yet it catches an amazing number of balls. It is now a part of golfing history that when Mr. Leslie Balfour-Melville won the amateur championship he beat successively at the nineteenth hole Mr. W. Greig, Mr. Laurence Auchterlonie, and Mr. John Ball, and all three of these redoubtable persons plumped the ball into this apparently paltry little streamlet with their approach shots.

The second is a beautiful hole some four hundred yards in length, and with the most destructive of pot-bunkers close up against the hole. Here is a case in point, when the attempt to shave narrowly past the bunker involves terrible risks, and it is the part of prudence to play well out to the right and trust to the long putt. There are, indeed, those who deem the hole unfairly difficult when it is cut in the left-hand end of the green and quite close to the bunker; I have not sufficient experience or pugnacity to argue with them.

The third is something similar in character, though shorter in length; while the fourth again is a little longer. Indeed there is something in these three holes that make them quite ridiculously difficult for the stranger to disentangle one from the other. The fourth is guarded in front by a small grassy mound, which has a wonderfully far-reaching effect, since wherever we may place our drive the mound must needs play some part in our calculations as to the second shot. I should add that at all three of these holes a tee-shot that is badly sliced will be caught in the fringe of rough ground that divides the old course from the new; this rough, however, is not so severe as it once

170

was, and would be none the worse for a little artificial assistance in the way of bunkers.

The fifth is the long hole out, when we shall need our three strokes to reach the green, which stands a little above us on a plateau of magnificent dimensions, where we rub shoulders with the incoming couples who are plying the 'Hole o' Cross.' In ancient days, when the whins were thick and flourishing on the straight road to the hole, the only possible line was away to the left towards the Elysian fields. It was from there, so Mr. James Cunningham has told me, that young Tommy Morris astonished the spectators by taking his niblick, a club that in those days had a face of about the magnitude of a half-crown, wherewith to play a pitch on the green. Till that historic moment no one had ever dreamed of a niblick being used for anything but ordinary spade work.

At the heathery hole we have a fine sea of whins on our right (there are still some whins left at St. Andrews), although only a very bad slice will make us acquainted with them; there are furthermore some pots on the left to trap a pulled ball, but altogether the hole is, if one may venture to say so, of no enormous merit, and by no means as good as the High Hole, where is a green of horrible glassy slopes and bunkers that eat their way voraciously into its borders.

At the eighth we do at last get a chance of a three, for the hole is a short one—142 yards long to be precise—and there is a fair measure of room on the green. So far the golf has been very, very good indeed, but with the ninth and tenth come two holes that constitute a small blot on the fair fame of the course. If they were found on some less sacred spot they would be condemned as consisting of a drive and a pitch up and down a flat field. What makes it the sadder is that ready to the architect's hand is a bit of glorious golfing country on the confines of the new course. However, we had better play these two holes in as reverent a spirit as possible and be thankful for two fairly easy fours, because the next is the 'short hole in,' and we must reserve all our energies for that. The only consoling thing about the hole is that the green slopes upward, so that it is not quite so easy for the ball to run over it as it otherwise would be. This is really but cold comfort, however, because the danger of going too far is not so imminent as that of not going straight enough. There is one bunker called 'Strath,' which is to the right, and there is another called the 'Shelly Bunker,' to the left; there is also another bunker short of Strath to catch the thoroughly short and ineffective ball. The hole is as a rule cut fairly close to Strath, wherefore it behoves the careful man to play well away to the left, and not to take undue risks by going straight for the hole. This may sound pusillanimous, but trouble once begun at this hole may never come to an end till the card is torn into a thousand fragments. With a stout niblick shot the ball may easily be dislodged from Strath, but it will all too probably bound over the green into the sandy horrors of the Eden. From there it may again be extracted, but as it has to pitch on a down slope, it will almost certainly trickle gently down the green till it is safely at rest once more in the bosom of Strath. This very tragedy I saw befall Massy in the Championship of 1910, and he took six to the hole. Many a good golfer has taken far more strokes than that, and, indeed, it is a hole to leave behind one with a sigh of satisfaction.

The next hole would in any case fall almost inevitably flat, but the thirteenth, the Hole o' Cross, is a great hole, where having struck two really fine shots and escaped 'Walkinshaw's Grave,' we may hope to reach the beautiful big plateau green in two and hole out in two more. The long hole home comes next, and here we drive along the Elysian fields, taking care to avoid a swarm of little pot-bunkers on the left, which are called the 'Beardies.' A second, played cautiously away to the left, will very likely bring us into collision with some outgoing couple, while a bold shot straight ahead of us may see the ball plump down into 'Hell,' a bunker that is now hardly worthy of its name. There is a pretty approach to be played, with yet another plateau to climb, and a five means good work, as does a four at the fifteenth, which is a thoroughly admirable two-shot hole.

Although home is now in sight, there are yet two terribly dangerous holes to be played. First of all we must steer down the perilously narrow space between the 'Principal's Nose' and the railway line—the railway line, mark you, that is not out of bounds, so that there is no limit to the number of strokes that we may spend in hammering vainly at an insensate sleeper. We may, of course, drive safe away to the left, and if our score is a good one we shall be

173

wise to do so, but our approach, as is only fair, will then be the more difficult, and there are bunkers lurking by the green-side.

The seventeenth hole has been more praised and more abused probably than any other hole in the world. It has been called unfair, and by many harder names as well; it has caused champions with a predilection for pitching rather than running to tear their hair; it has certainly ruined an infinite number of scores. Many like it, most respect it, and all fear it. First there is the tee-shot, with the possibility of slicing out of bounds into the station-master's garden or pulling into various bunkers on the left. Then comes the second, a shot which should not entail immediate disaster, but which is nevertheless of enormous importance as leading up to the third. Finally, there is the approach to that little plateau—in contrast to most of the St. Andrews greens, a horribly small and narrow one— that lies between a greedy little bunker on the one side and a brutally hard road on the other. It is so difficult as to make the boldest inclined to approach on the instalment system, and yet no amount of caution can do away with the chance of disaster. There was a harrowing moment in the Championship of 1910 when Braid's ball lay in the little bunker under the green. Even if he got it safely out, it was practically certain he would be two strokes behind Duncan, with one round to go; if he did not get it out, or got it out too far and so on to the road, his chances would be terribly jeopardized. It was, as I say, an agonizing moment, but no one plays the heavy 'dunch' shot out of sand quite so surely as Braid. Down came the niblick, up spouted the sand, and out came the ball, to fall spent and lifeless close to the hole and out of reach of that cruel road.

After this hole of many disastrous memories, the eighteenth need have no great terrors. We drive over the burn, cross by the picturesque old stone bridge, and avoiding the grosser forms of sin, such as slicing into the windows of Rusack's hotel, hole out in four, or at most five, under the critical gaze of those that lean on the railings.

No account of St. Andrews would be complete without some mention of the new course, which runs more or less parallel with the old; the two, to say nothing of the Jubilee course that runs along the spurs of the sandhills, being all squeezed into a wonderfully narrow compass.

The new course has many merits, but it is curiously unlike its next-door neighbour. Partly, of course, this is on account of its youth. Myriads of feet have not trampled it into a state of adamantine hardness, and when the greens on the old course are keen and fiery, the new course remains soft, slow and easy. Besides this, however, there is another difference, in that the new course is infinitely more ordinary, and this comparative commonplaceness, if further inquired into, resolves itself largely into the fact that there are not nearly so many good natural greens. At both the third and the fifth there are plateau greens, and the latter especially has the quality—so characteristic of the old course—of demanding that the shot be played exactly right. Most of the greens, however, are quite

175

GOLF COURSES

ordinary, and lack that priceless gift of being naturally protected by their own conformation.

Mr. Low has written that "the new course is probably the second course in Scotland," but I cannot help thinking that here he is a little too enthusiastic. If we were to light upon the course somewhere else than at St. Andrews, no doubt we should do it ampler justice than we do now, when it is so completely overshadowed, but should we declare it better than Prestwick, to name only one other famous Scottish course? Personally I do not think so.

No doubt the new course does suffer some considerable injustice, and always will do so. It has 'relief course' plainly written all over it. On the last occasion on which I played there the daisies were growing freely, and daisies, though extremely charming things in themselves, are not pleasant to putt over, and do not give a workman-like air to a course. It is a pity, because it is a good course, and we should be delighted to play over it anywhere else, but with the old course there—well, it is a waste of time.

Still there occasionally comes a time when we grow sick to death of the crowding and waiting on the old course, and then we are glad enough to steal away on to the new course and have a round, which will probably be at anyrate a comparatively quick one. We cross the burn; walk through the middle of the putting course, where are many ladies armed with wooden putters (since the sacrilegious cleek is wholly forbidden), and tee off not far from where they are playing to the second hole on the old course.

The first two holes are not at all exciting, but the course

improves as we go along. Three is a good hole, and five is an excellent short one, with a most difficult iron-shot on to a plateau green. Nine, again, is rather an attractive little hole, although there are two opinions about this; a very accurate drive between bents and sand, followed by rather a blind pitch on to a sunk green. Personally I like it, though it is not at all the type of hole one expects to find at St. Andrews, nor, for that matter, is the tenth. This is nevertheless a really fine one, running down a narrow gorge between two ranges of hills, with a fine, slashing second shot with the brassey, albeit more or less a blind one. The twelfth is as good as the eleventh is weak, and sixteen and eighteen are both long and difficult, but the two short holes, thirteen and seventeen, are decidedly not exciting. Quite good, difficult golf it is, but the " second course in Scotland "—no. Perhaps it might be, but, my dear Mr. Low, I am sure on reflection you will admit that, in fact, it isn't.

Though St. Andrews naturally enough dwarfs them all, there are other courses, and fine courses, in Fife. There is Elie, which has produced at least three very great golfers indeed, Douglas Rolland, Jack Simpson and James Braid; and there are also, amongst others, Crail and Leven. Leven, a truly charming course, has, alas! ceased to exist in its old form. Nine of the old holes now belong to a new and reconstituted Leven, and the other nine belong to Lundin Links. It is a sad pity, but the difficulty of two different starting places made it in these crowded times inevitable.

GOLF COURSES

Forfarshire, too, is a county of many courses. Barry, Broughty Ferry, Edzell, Monifieth, Montrose, and, best known of all, Carnoustie. **Carnoustie** is comparatively unknown, save by name, to the English golfer, but very popular indeed in its own country. So much so that its popularity has rendered necessary an auxiliary course, and the auxiliary course has taken a piece of good golfing ground that could ill be spared. It is a fine, big, open sandy seaside course; very natural in appearance; and in places, indeed, natural almost to the verge of roughness; but it is none the worse for that, however, and indeed it is altogether a very delightful course.

There is one curious feature, in that the taking in of some new ground has caused one hole to be of a completely inland character. Certainly this hole seems at first sight to be dragged in by the heels, but we readily forgive it its inland character, because it is really a very good hole indeed. This is number seven, ' South America ' by name. It is a good long hole, well over four hundred yards in length, and the green is on an island guarded by a ditch. The soil is completely inland in character—the green once formed part of an old garden—and as if to emphasize that fact, a solitary tree has been left as a hazard, and naturally plays a prominent part in the landscape.

Burns, *anglicé* streams, are a great feature of Carnoustie, Indeed one friend of mine returned from a visit there declaring that he had got burns badly on his nerves, and that the entire course was irrigated by them. However, it is not so much burns as sandhills that are likely to cause

178

CARNOUSTIE

'*South America*'

our downfall at the beginning. Of these hilly holes, the second, by name the 'Valley,' is a really fine one, and decidedly one of the best on the course. It is dog-legged in character, and has a distinct flavour of some of the holes at Prince's, since with the tee-shot the player carries just as much of the hill in front of him as he dares, and gains a proper advantage for a bold and successful shot. The drive is directed towards a guide flag on a hill top, and if all goes well we are over in the valley. Then follows a beautiful second shot up a narrow neck, with a bunker on the left and other trouble on the right; 385 yards is the Valley's length, and Bogey does the hole in four. It is certainly one of the holes that he plays in his best form, for he very often takes five over holes that are no longer and not nearly so difficult or so interesting. Of the other holes on the way out, most are decidedly long, except the fifth, which is a simple enough short hole, and 'South America,' before described, is as good as any of them.

On the way home there is a somewhat awe-inspiring second shot at the tenth, where we have to carry a hill, out of the face of which two bunkers have been cut out and appropriately christened the 'Spectacles.' The twelfth has a pleasing name, 'Jockey's Burn,' and the thirteenth has a pleasing putting green. The fourteenth, by name the 'Flagstaff,' is a good long and narrow hole, where the hills crowd in close upon us, and we must keep straight along the valley. The best hole on the way home, however, is probably the sixteenth, or 'Island,' where there is but one way to secure an easy and comfortable approach, and that consists of pushing your tee-shot out to the right so that the ball comes to rest upon a very narrow neck. Take an easier route from the tee, and you will be left with as unpleasant a pitch as need be, and the greedy waters of a burn running between you and the hole. Burns play an important part at both the last two holes also, for one has to be carried from the seventeenth tee and another menaces the pitch on to the home green. There really is some justification for the nervous golfer who has water on the brain after a round at Carnoustie.

CHAPTER XI.

THE COURSES OF THE EAST LOTHIAN AND EDINBURGH.

THERE is probably no other golfing centre that is quite so good as **Gullane,** in the East Lothian. If the golfer can only get up early enough in the morning, and has the strength to do it, he can play on seven courses on one long summer's day. At his very door is a trinity of courses—Gullane, New Gullane, and New Luffness—which, to the eye of the stranger, are indistinguishable the one from the other. From Gullane Hill to the Luffness Club-house is one huge stretch of turf, and such turf! the finest, smoothest, and most delicate that ever was seen. It has been said of various people—I do not know who was the original subject—that nobody could be so wise as so-and-so looked; likewise, it might be said that no greens could be so good as the Gullane and Luffness greens look. Nevertheless, they are very good indeed, and so is the golf.

Till quite lately there was a marked distinction between the two Gullane courses. The new course was long, testing, and difficult; the old course was a place of divine

181

putting greens and pretty pitching shots; but it made no great demands on the athletic powers of its devotees. There was no more delightful course in the world for those whose game consists, to quote the *Golfer's Manual*, written in 1857, in "Spooning a ball gently on to a table of smooth turf, when a longer shot would land them in grief." Now all this has been changed—the course has burst forth into new life and length, and its older and gentler and, possibly, more lovable qualities have gone. It was inevitable that there should be some to regret the change, but the result is now that the visitor to Gullane has two really fine, difficult courses at his own front door, both over 6000 yards long. The old course runs right down to the sea, and there are fine views of the Firth of Forth, while, from the new course, we look at another charming view in Aberlady Bay.

Close to the two Gullane courses, a little further in the direction of Aberlady, is New Luffness, another admirable course. Here we must keep most particularly straight, for the fairway is narrow, and there is plenty of rough at the sides, including some particularly pernicious objects (I am no botanist, and do not know their names) which have tall, wiry stalks and sadly impede the club.

It is really a beautiful bit of natural golfing country, and we are far enough away from the houses of Gullane to enjoy a perfect sense of peace and quietude. Not far off, again, is Kilspindie, on the west side of Aberlady Bay, another charming spot where we may play golf that is good without being too desperately difficult.

GULLANE

The sixth green and seventh tee

EAST LOTHIAN AND EDINBURGH

We must get back to Gullane, however, where at the far end of the village, on the road to North Berwick, is a course of greater fame than any of those I have mentioned —**Muirfield,** the home of the Honourable Company of Edinburgh golfers, and one of the select band of championship courses. Muirfield has had rather a chequered career in regard to public estimation, and has been at different times very violently abused, partly because the Honourable Company, in leaving Musselburgh, took the championship with them away from its ancient home : partly on account of the intrinsic merits or demerits of the links. The Open Championship was for the first time played at Muirfield in 1892, and it is possible that the course was hardly good enough or long enough for a championship course. Certainly the score with which the championship was won was phenomenally low for those days of gutty balls. It was altogether a memorable championship, for several reasons; it marked the beginning of the decline of Musselburgh, it was played for the first time over 72 instead of 36 holes, and it was won by an amateur, Mr. Hilton. That change from one to two days' play may be said to have robbed another great amateur of the honour of being open champion, for at the end of the first day Mr. Horace Hutchinson had a handsome lead. On the second day, alas ! an unfortunate encounter with that fatal wood at the very first hole was the beginning of a series of disasters. There is always something bitterly hard about being the first to suffer through a reform, however excellent it may be in the abstract, and I have always felt dreadfully sorry for Mr. Hutchinson.

GOLF COURSES

However, one amateur's loss was another's gain, and Mr. Hilton, after being eight strokes behind on the first day, came away with a wonderful game on the second, nearly doing the first hole in one, holing two pitches, and racing so fast round the course as nearly to be the death of an ancient partner. It is interesting to read in Mr. Hilton's reminiscences that it was only two days before the event that he decided to enter for this momentous championship, and that his course of training consisted of three rounds in one day immediately following a night journey. Here is a fine chance for a confusion of thought between cause and effect.

Muirfield has been a good deal altered since then, and, if it will never be among the most prepossessing of courses, it is now both sound and interesting, while, given any appreciable amount of wind, it is thoroughly difficult. It is curious that it has but little outward attractions. There is a fine view of the sea and a delightful sea wood, with the trees all bent and twisted by the wind; then, too, it is a solitary and peaceful spot, and a great haunt of the curlews, whom one may see hovering over a championship crowd and crying eerily amid a religious silence. All this is charming, but there is a fatal stone wall that runs round the course, giving the impression of an inland park, and it is, I believe, this purely sentimental objection that has brought Muirfield so many detractors. Not that there are not or have not been other objections of a more practical kind. The course has twice had to be lengthened, and there was, moreover, a time when the ground near the

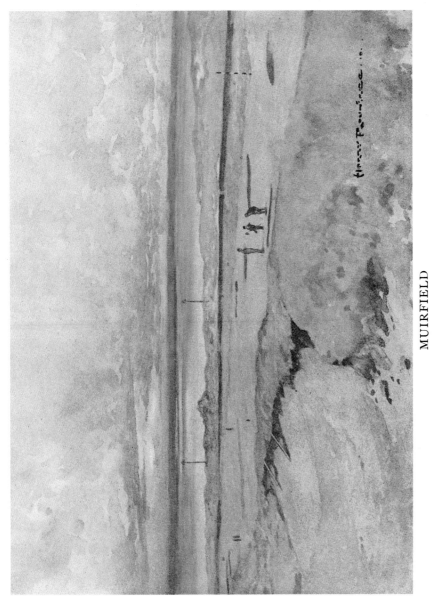

MUIRFIELD

The fourth and fourteenth greens

edges of the greens was very spongy and uncertain in character. The greens are rather small—this is entirely a virtue—and, consequently, there are many little chips and running shots to be played; these, when the greens were hard and the surrounding country was soft, were apt to travel upon the wings of chance, and there were many lamentations. Now, however, the ground has hardened considerably, and at the last Amateur Championship there were no complaints on this score, although the greens themselves were difficult and, indeed, almost tricky.

On a calm day it may be urged that there are not enough long second shots, and that there are too many holes of rather similar length, which can be reached with a drive and a moderate pitching shot. Certainly, on the very still, warm days that preceded the Amateur Championship of 1909, the golf appeared rather easy, and every self-respecting person was coming in to lunch having done his 75 or 76, but as soon as any breeze sprang up, there was a very different story to tell. For one thing, the tee-shots in a wind impose a continual strain. Sunningdale, Walton Heath, Worplesdon, and other inland courses have their endless avenues of heather and fir trees, but at none of them, I fancy, is the fairway quite so narrow as at Muirfield, and a whole round without a single tee-shot going astray into the rough is something to be proud of. I have heard one of the most accomplished of wooden club players confess that a week at Muirfield had frightened him out of his driving, and only the ampler spaces of North Berwick gave him back his courage.

185

GOLF COURSES

The rough consists of thick, coarse grass, and there is, of course, a measure of chance in the lies that one may get; one may be able to use a brassey, but a niblick is infinitely the more likely club. When Mr. Herman de Zoete played so finely in the championship of 1903, it was said, mainly as an argument against the rubber ball, that he was never on the course at all, but it must be remembered that he was holing out quite wonderfully well, and he is, moreover, gifted with exceptional powers in the way of moving mountains of long grass. For weaker brethren many excursions into the rough are almost certain to be fatal.

Muirfield is one of the comparatively few courses that begin with a one-shot hole, with the result that the starting of a round is rather a slow business, since there is wood to the left and some alluring bunkers to the right, and the erratic are likely to be an unconscionable time a-playing. Never was there a greater necessity to resist the temptation to pull than there is at the second; instinct keeps calling in our ears for a glorious, long hook, and there is nothing so likely to prove fatal. It is one of those puzzling shots where we drive at a wide angle on to a narrow fairway, whence, if all goes well, a good iron shot will land the ball on to a very well-guarded green, fast in pace and billowy in conformation. It is a capital four-hole, and so is the third, which is really a splendid example of how good a hole of no particular length can be. In the first place, we must hit straight, and we must also be exceedingly careful not to hit too far. If, indeed, we can send

186

the ball flying like an arrow from the bow, we may make for the little narrow neck, where safety lies; but it is far more probable that our ball will trickle gently down hill to the left, where a stream and a surrounding marsh await it. Save, therefore, when with a strong wind behind we may hope to get over all our troubles with one vast blow, we must play prudently from the tee with an iron club, and we shall still be able to reach the green very comfortably in our second. It is a slippery, elusive, and vindictive sort of green, however, full of unexpected quicknesses and slownesses, and it is one thing to be there in two and quite another to be down in four : altogether a very interesting hole to see played by somebody else.

Of the next few holes, the fifth is perhaps the outstanding one, on account of its length : the others are all of them good and all of them, as regards length, much of a muchness. We remember a different feature at each of them— the big carry over the boarded bunker at the sixth, the pond at the seventh, and the tall sandhill, rising rather abruptly in front of the tee, at the ninth—but we generally have the same iron club in our hands for the second shot. At the eleventh, however, we come to a really splendid hole, at which each shot has infinite terrors. The tee-shot has to be played down a narrow spit of land, with thick, rough grass on the right, a bunker encroaching on the left, and a continuation of the same bunker straight ahead of us. Nor must the ubiquitous wall, also on the left, be entirely despised. The very least hook will plunge us into the left-hand end of the bunker, a slice means the long grass, and a very long, straight ball may go too far and meet a sandy fate. The shot is so narrow and frightening that it is no sign of cowardice to take a cleek, but then a very long second shot is necessary, unless the wind is strong behind, in order to get home. This second shot, too, is fraught with almost equal perils, for the wall to the left comes very decidedly into the range of practical politics, and there is a long bunker to the right. It is a hole at which one need never despair, and I wish I could remember accurately the exact number of balls Mr. Harold Hambro hit over the wall in 1903 and yet won the hole from Mr. Edward Blackwell.

The twelfth needs a high carrying second over a deep bunker; and the thirteenth has one of the most terrifying tee-shots that I know along a narrow strath, with bunkers on either side. Moreover, not only is it necessary to hit straight, but it is intensely profitable to hit a long way, for if we can only hit far enough, we may play a running shot on to that sliding, sloping green, whereas if we have to pitch on to the slope over the corner of the right-hand bunker, a five is, to put it mildly, far more likely than a three. The fifteenth, again, is a beautiful drive and pitch hole, with a number of alternative routes, all of which want accurate hitting, and all leading up to a most difficult approach shot. At the sixteenth we play short of a huge cross-bunker in our second, unless we are taking serious risks; and at the seventeenth our second shot is once more a tricky pitch on to a sloping green. I do not think I ever saw a hole better played than Mr. Maxwell played this seventeenth in the final of the championship of 1909, when he stood one down with two to play. The only way in which he was in the least likely to get the three, that he needed so sorely, was to play his pitch along a certain gully that led to the hole. In order to get at that gully, he had to play his tee-shot well away to the left, keeping as close as he dared to the left-hand rough. He played the shot perfectly, ' pinching ' the rough successfully, and was left with a pitch straight up the gully : played that perfectly too : was left with a putt of some four feet, and holed it. The strokes were so clearly intended, and so bravely played, and in all human probability they made the difference between Mr. Maxwell winning or losing the championship.

Finally, the last hole is a good, honest, two-shot hole straight up to the club-house, with a trench bunker right across the course. In respect to this hole, golfing history gives rather an interesting example of the difference between the gutty and the rubber-core. When Vardon won his first championship, he was left, at this hole, with a four to win and a five to tie with Taylor. He debated long over his second shot, and then played short with his iron, got his five, and made sure of the tie—a tie which, as all the world knows, he won. Nowadays, comparatively modest hitters often get home with iron clubs, and it would need a very stiff wind to deter Vardon from attacking that big bunker with his second. It is rather salutary for us sometimes to be reminded of how much we owe to the rubber-cored ball, and Muirfield is a course that is continually dinning the fact into our ears. There are so many holes there that would be so much harder for the moderate driver if he had to drive a solid ball; he could be dreadfully out of conceit with himself at the end of the round.

It is quite a short drive—not with a club—from Muirfield **to North Berwick**, but there is none of that resemblance between the courses that one might expect between such near neighbours. Muirfield may be called a narrow course of soft turf; North Berwick an open course of hard turf. Moreover, one may chance to have Muirfield to one's self and the curlews, whereas at North Berwick are to be found all the advantages or disadvantages of a fashionable watering-place. Whatever may be thought of their respective merits from a strictly golfing point of view, it can hardly be gainsayed that North Berwick has the best of it in point of looks. No golf course could look lovelier than North Berwick on a bright summer's day, when the Bass rock, the home of many gannets, is shining brilliantly white in the sunshine and only holiday-making man is entirely vile.

No course has ever undergone a more complete metamorphosis, for whereas it is now long enough for any reasonable person, it was once noted for the abnormal number of threes that could be done in one round. Mr. Hutchinson wrote in the Badminton of the "sporting little links of North Berwick," and added "You might just as well leave your driver at home. If you are even a medium driver, it is scarcely ever in your hand." Incredible

190

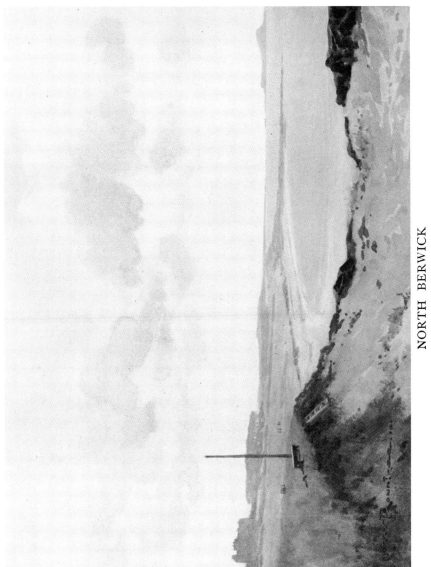

NORTH BERWICK

The second tee

scores were recorded by Mr. Laidlay and Bernard Sayers, perhaps the most astounding being Mr. Laidlay's 33 for the first ten holes. Such a course was almost bound to produce a race of wonderfully adroit pitchers. Of the older generation, Mr. Laidlay and Sayers are still almost as good as ever, and the race of fine pitchers is not extinct, for amongst others there is Mr. Maxwell, whose obvious power rather blinds the unobservant eye to his beautiful short game; and Mr. Whitecross, a player much less well known, but a wonderfully deft wielder of the mashie. Mr. Whitecross's pitching at Muirfield in 1909 more nearly approached the supernatural than anything I have ever seen. If I remember aright, he actually holed two pitches in his matches with Mr. Angus Hambro and Mr. W. A. Henderson, and laid the ball several times on the lip of the hole; one shot in particular against Mr. Hambro, wherein the ball trickled very slowly down the steep slope of the seventeenth green and lay absolutely dead, was the most perfect shot conceivable, and was played, besides, at an intensely critical moment.

It would seem, therefore, that though North Berwick is no longer short, it is still an exceptionally good school in which to learn the art of approaching. There is even now a good deal of approaching to do, and the man who is driving well may hope to reach the green fairly often with pitching shots of varying length. For these shots not only is plenty of skill essential, but a measure of local knowledge is also useful, and the unaccustomed stranger is apt to think and say that it is possible in two successive

GOLF COURSES

rounds to play the approach shots equally well with vastly different results.

Personally, I have a considerable respect for North Berwick, born of fear and conscious incompetence. I always have that respectful feeling towards a course where the ground is a little hard and bumpy. Given soft, velvety turf, one should be able, to a certain extent, to disguise one's weakness, for it is then an easy matter to get the ball well into the air, and the short putts may be firmly hit. When the turf is bare, one has to do all the work one's self, and though North Berwick has not the uncompromising hardness of St. Andrews, neither has it any of the kindly and flattering qualities of Sandwich. The unheeding multitude cut out many divots and leave a good many difficult lies behind them, and the ball will very easily run away from one on the putting green; indeed, at Point Garry, it is apt, if too vigorously struck, to run into the sea.

It is a terrible place this double green of Point Garry, worn, bare, and sloping down to the rocks and the beach, and we come to it, besides, at two of the most agitating moments of the round; at the first hole, when we have not had quite enough golf, and at the seventeenth, when, if the match has been a fierce one, we have perhaps had too much. Our terror is perhaps less acute at the first hole, because we are then playing on the part of the green that is furthest from the sea; but even so great trouble may befall us. I always remember a newspaper account of Mr. Balfour, when he was Prime Minister, playing in a

192

medal at North Berwick. "The premier," so it ran, "made an unfortunate start : put his second on the rocks and took eight to the hole." We ought, generally speaking, to do better than eight; indeed, we may hope for a three—that is to say, if we are playing from the forward tee, and the wind is not against us. Then we carry the road and reach the green in one most excellent shot, but if the circumstances are at all unfavourable, we shall doubtless do better to play short from the tee with an iron club and be well content with a four.

The second and third are both fine holes, and at the second we have an added interest in the possibility of killing some one upon the sea-shore. With a fine long shot we may hope to carry a portion of the beach that eats its way into the course, but it is not well to be too adventurous; anything approaching a slice will leave us playing niblick shots among the pebbles and nurserymaids, and we can play reasonably well to the left and yet hope to get home next time with a well-struck second. At the third, when we carry the wall in our second, we may be content with a five, though a four is not impossible, and then a rather unusual hazard awaits us at the hole called 'Carl Kemp.' If we drive straight we shall have a sufficiently easy pitch to play, but the green lies in a narrow pass, with rocks on either side, and no one can predict the fate of a ball that pitches upon a rock; it may bound incredibly both as regards distance and direction.

Soon after this we get into a country of flat and, if the truth be told, rather dull holes. Of the holes at this end of the course, it may be said that they are good enough when the wind is against, but they never can be very thrilling. Even the quarry and the eel burn, though they help to fix them in the mind, cannot make us love them very passionately; and as for the ninth, when we drive down to the edge of a cross-bunker and then chip over on to the green, that, I vow, is a thoroughly commonplace and uninteresting hole. It has some compensation to offer, in that it is the chosen pitch of a purveyor of ginger beer; it was here that the famous Crawford used to abide, and no hole could be entirely dull with Crawford on the tee.

It is not till we reach the wall that we come to a hole that makes a very strong appeal to the imagination. Here we shall have to play a cunning little pitch in our best North Berwick manner, for the green lies immediately beyond the wall, and we must contrive to stop the ball reasonably dead with our mashie. We can, however, make the shot more or less difficult, according as we drive well or ill. If we can hold the ball well to the left—close, but not too close under the wall—we shall have more room to pitch, and may hope for a putt for three; but a drive pushed far out to the right makes it almost impossible to stop at all near the hole next time.

'Perfection' and 'The Redan' are two very famous names, and the 'Redan' is one of the select holes, the features of which have been more or less faithfully reproduced on the National Golf Course on Long Island, U.S.A. First of the two comes 'Perfection,' the fourteenth, a very fine two-shot hole. With the tee-shot we must hug as closely as we dare the side of a big hill on the left, and if we fall into the opposite extreme, we may slice our ball among the rocks of 'Carl Kemp.' All being well, we have a reasonably easy second over a bunker; but we cannot see where we are going, and have the uncanny feeling that we are hitting straight into the sea. The 'Redan' is a beautiful one-shot hole on the top of a plateau, with a bunker short of the green to the left and another further on to the right, and we must vary our mode of attack according to the wind, playing a shot to come in from the right or making a direct frontal attack.

At the sixteenth we cross the wall once more, and may hope to reach in two shots the 'Gate' hole, standing on another plateau—an exceedingly diminutive one, by the way—close to the high road. Now we arrive at that most destructive of holes, 'Point Garry,' and even if we do not, like Mr. Balfour, make an unfortunate start, we are very likely to make an unfortunate ending. In our second shot we shall have to decide whether or not to carry a bunker that stretches across our path, and then comes the crucial shot, the approach on to that dreadful green that slopes right away from us to the sea—without the ghost of a charitable back wall. It is so frightening that we are strongly tempted to approach it on the instalment system, and it is really wonderful how many instalments may be necessary, as with limbs palsied with terror, we push and poke the ball over that treacherous and slippery surface. 'Point Garry' safely over, the last hole seems absurdly simple, and, if we do not top into the road or pull into

GOLF COURSES

Hutchison's shop, we should end with a four; indeed, our putt for a possible three should not be a very long one. When all is over, we shall almost certainly agree that the best golf at North Berwick is to be found at the beginning and end of the course, but we could hardly bear it if all the holes were as exciting as 'Point Garry.' Those flat holes at the far end serve, no doubt, a useful, though unobtrusive, purpose.

So much for the East Lothian courses, but while we are within hail of Edinburgh, we must pay a visit to **Musselburgh**, the home of the Parks and once the home of the championship, now shorn of its honour, and little more than a name to English golfers. The way to Musselburgh lies for the most part through factory chimneys and slag heaps, nor is the first glimpse of the course much more prepossessing than the surrounding scenery. It looks like an ordinary common on the outskirts of a town, rather flat, and devoid of features, rather hard and rough, not unlike in character that blank stretch of turf at St. Andrews which lies between the club-house and the burn. Yet if, after we have played over the course, we adhere to this our first view, we shall show ourselves to be persons of superficial minds and of little discernment. It is true that there are comparatively few hazards, and that we ought, therefore, not to get into many of them; but, at the same time, it will gradually dawn upon us that nearly every hole has a governing hazard, to which we must pay due regard—one that will direct our policy for us whether we like it or not. We must not let ourselves be lulled into

MUSSELBURGH

'Mrs, Forman's'

a sense of false security by the fact that we have occasionally a whole parish to drive into. There is a right line and a wrong line, and if we are very fortunate, or very highly honoured, we may have it pointed out to us and our clubs carried for us by Bob Ferguson, who won the championship three times running, and might have won it a fourth time if Willy Fernie had not done the last hole at Musselburgh in two.

There are but nine holes at Musselburgh, and the whole area of the links is extremely small. The first three holes go along the entire length of the course on the right-hand side; then comes one hole across, four down the left side, and then one more across the other end. Of these nine, the first three are as good holes as you can desire to meet anywhere, whether you play them with a stone-hard gutty, as did the reverent pilgrims of the Oxford and Cambridge Golfing Society, or with the soft and bounding rubber-core. The first rejoices in the cheerful name of the 'Graves,' owing to the conformation of the putting green, which, with its many little barrows, is like a grass-grown burial-ground. Here two good shots should reach the green, and two very good putts may reach the bottom of the hole. For the second we shall need a five, although a vast hitter may get home with two of his very best. The green is a small plateau at the end of a valley that is long and shallow and narrow, and if we can place the ball with our second shot on exactly the right place, we should have an easy run up and a putt for four; if we are not in the right place, we must play a difficult approach well in order to get a five.   Next comes another hole with a famous name—'Mrs. Forman's'—and we approach Mrs. Forman's tavern with two shots to the left, followed by a run up, or—more perilously—by two shots on the dead straight line.   By the latter method we may, indeed, get home in two, but we may also be under the posts of the race-course or in an electric tram-car, or in a variety of bunkers, and it may be added that they do not pamper us at Musselburgh by raking the bunkers or trimming the steep over-hanging cliffs thereof.

The fourth is a long one-shot hole in a seaward direction, and the next is 'Pandy.'   'Pandy' itself is now a flat, ugly bit of hard, dirty sand, and if we do get into it, we should lie well enough to get a long way out again, unless, indeed, we should be so unfortunate as to lie in a tin-pot or a derelict boot.   The green is one of which Willy Park has made two famous copies—one at the fifteenth at Huntercombe, the other the eighth at Worplesdon. Whereas, however, there is usually a generous growth of velvety grass on the Huntercombe green, the original green at Musselburgh is of a terrifying keenness.   The seventh is a shortish hole of no great interest, and the eighth is the 'Gas Works,' which can be reached with a drive and a run up, and has a green which, like most of the others at Musselburgh, seems to accentuate any putting error in an exemplary fashion.   Finally, for the ninth and last, there is another short hole, having a big plateau green protected in front by a wavy bank.   Some will play to pitch at the bottom of the bank and run up; others to toss the ball

EAST LOTHIAN AND EDINBURGH

high and boldly on to the green. The latter is probably preferable for those whose ambition does not soar above a three, but those who spurn safety and aim at twos will adopt the former plan. Thus ends Musselburgh, which can be compassed in some 35 strokes or less, but will probably cost us appreciably more, for neither the lies nor the greens are easy, and it is extremely easy to drop strokes.

To the English golfer there is something incongruous in the idea of an inland course in Scotland. He goes there for his holidays, and so naturally chooses a seaside course; but Scotland possesses a number of inhabitants who are not always making holiday, and cannot go to the sea as often as they would like, wherefore the necessity for this seeming incongruity. Of the inland Scottish courses, probably the best known is **Barnton,** near Edinburgh, the home of a golf club of great antiquity and renown, the Edinburgh Burgess Golfing Society, who rank in seniority second only to the Royal Blackheath Club.

The Barnton estate consists of a fine old house and a park, with splendid trees, which was once known as Cramond Regis, and was a hunting seat of the kings of Scotland. From royalty it passed successively into the hands of several noble Scottish families, till it fell into those of the Edinburgh Burgesses, when they decided to leave Musselburgh. That move took place in comparatively modern times, but before that golf had been played in the park by at least one very distinguished golfer, Robert Clark, who wrote *Golf: a Royal and Ancient Game.* He was at one time tenant of Barnton House, and, as I

199

GOLF COURSES

learn from an interesting article by Mr. James Purves, had some holes cut, including one which necessitated a drive right over the house. When he was annoyed with his game at Musselburgh, he would declare that he had a far better course at his own door.

Whether he would have upheld that pronouncement in cool blood is perhaps to be doubted, for the best park golf in the world cannot attain beyond a certain point, and Barnton is pure park golf. Still, it has undoubtedly many merits, and not least among them is that the greens are as good and true as any in the world. That at least is the general opinion, and I see no reason to doubt it. I cannot, on the other hand, confirm it, because I have only played at Barnton on a Sunday, and the Scottish conscience, although it will let you play, will not let the greens be swept for you, and Sunday golf at Barnton, therefore, involves some encounters with worm casts. It also involves, or did when last I went there, a drive out of Edinburgh with one's clubs elaborately hidden under horse-cloths and rugs. The principle, however, was that of the ostrich who buries his head in the sand, or rather its exact converse, for the most sedulous burying of the bodies of the clubs did not prevent the head peeping out and so advising all church-going Edinburgh of one's scandalous project.

It is easy to see that on week days the course must be in absolutely apple-pie order, and that it lacks nothing that the hand of man could do for it. Nearly all the holes want good, straight, accurate play; but, as is the case with

200

BARNTON

Park golf in Scotland

this type of golf, they make no passionate appeal to the imagination. There is a nice tee-shot from a height at the ninth, where two really good shots down a valley should take us home; and the eleventh, sixteenth, and seventeenth all want long and straight hitting. At the thirteenth a pleasing variety is introduced in the matter of hazards by two old tombstones, which may catch a badly pulled ball. These, according to Mr. Purves, are memorials of an over-flow from the parish churchyard at Cramond at the time of the plague.

Barnton is a great resort of the lawyers of Edinburgh, and there is a nice little joke with a legal flavour to it at the end of the candidate's application for membership, wherein, after declaring that he is an "ardent admirer and player of the ancient and manly game of golf," he concludes, "and your petitioner will ever play." What is more, he has got to play in his club uniform, a red coat and a black velvet cap—he is fined if he doesn't—and very pretty the red coats look on a summer day amid the pleasant greenery of Barnton.

CHAPTER XII.

WEST OF SCOTLAND: PRESTWICK AND TROON.

GULLANE is usually cited as the headquarters from which
it is possible to play the largest number of rounds in one
day, each round being on a different course, but it is by
no means certain that the distinction which is thus given
to East Lothian does not really belong to Prestwick and
Troon. As one approaches Prestwick, the train seems to
be voyaging through one endless and continuous golf
course—Gailes, Barassie, Bogside—I write them down
pell-mell as they come into my head—Prestwick, St.
Nicholas, St. Cuthbert, Troon, and several more beside.
Moreover, Troon "surprises by himself," a prodigious
assemblage of courses. There is the course proper, and
there is the 'relief' course; there is another course, which
may be termed the 'super-relief' course; and there are
various practice grounds consecrated to women and children. The turf is something softer—at least in my
imagination—than that of the East Coast courses, and the
greens are wonderfully green and velvety, and looking as
if they get plenty of rain, as in fact they do.

PRESTWICK AND TROON

Of all this galaxy of courses, **Prestwick** is first and foremost. It is the original home of the Open Championship, one of the championship courses of to-day, and admittedly one of the best of them. A man is probably less likely to be contradicted in lauding Prestwick than in singing the praises of any other course in Christendom. There are probably more people who would put St. Andrews absolutely at the top of the tree, but, whereas nearly everyone would rank Prestwick in the first three, the Fifeshire course has a certain number of bitter enemies who rank it very low indeed. One might almost say that Prestwick has no enemies; everyone admires it, though, naturally, with slightly different degrees of enthusiasm. To say of a human being that he has no enemies is almost to insinuate that he is just a little bit colourless and insipid; but those adjectives have certainly no application to Prestwick, which has a very decided character of its own.

Nowhere is to be found a more beautiful stretch of what is called "natural golfing country." The ordinary golfer, whose head is not too full of modern architectural ideas, would jump with joy on first beholding Prestwick. There is nothing subtle or recondite about it; it has a beauty which explains itself. There are the great sandhills bristling with bents and the little nestling valleys beyond them, a rushing burn and a stone wall, and it is perfectly clear that man was meant to hit the ball over them. All the ground on the near side of the wall, which is the ground of the old twelve-hole course, is of this glorious 'natural' character. "Hullo," says the player, "here's a hill:

203

let's drive over it." Yet, although it is a little blind and has a measure of what Mr. Hutchinson has euphemistically termed "pleasurable uncertainty," it is for the most part incontestibly fine golf. "Like Sandwich, only much better," I have heard it described; but I dislike this slandering and backbiting at poor, dear Sandwich. In one respect, however, it may be permissible to make a comparison very much in favour of Prestwick, that is in the size of the greens. On both courses we hit the ball over a high hill, but whereas at Prestwick we must hit it straight, unless we wish to be left with the trickiest and hardest of little pitches, at Sandwich a far more than reasonably crooked shot may yet land the ball on the edge of a vast green, where a bang with the wooden putter will make up for our deficiencies.

When once the wall is crossed, and what was once called the new ground is reached, the character of the ground changes considerably. There are, it is true, two blind and mountainous tee-shots over the famous 'Himalayas,' but they appear rather esoteric than otherwise. The holes on the far side of the wall are in their nature essentially flat, and in one or two instances a little artificial. As one plays the eighth hole alongside the railway by Monkton Station, one cannot repress the feeling that one might as well have stayed inland. Well bunkered and difficult enough is that particular hole, and yet so utterly lacking in the least breath of the sea, and the fairway is just a smooth avenue mowed out of a big field. Still some others of these flattish holes—I shall come to them in their proper places—are

PRESTWICK

Looking back at the ' Alps '

undoubtedly very fine holes, and if anyone likes to say that they are in reality better golf than those within the wall, we may still respect his judgment and regard him as a man and brother. Equally we may form a low estimate of his appreciation of the beautiful and romantic, and remain perfectly steadfast in our own allegiance to the 'Alps,' the 'Cardinal,' and the 'Sea-He'therick.'

The first hole is so good that, as with the first at Hoylake, it is a pity that we have to play it while we are still, perhaps, a little stiff and nervous. The crime against which we have chiefly to be on our guard is that of slicing, for the railway runs along the entire length of the hole on the right-hand side, quite unpleasantly near us. We must not hook either, for rough country awaits the ball hit unduly far to the left, and, indeed, the shot is such a narrow one that there are some strong hitters who advocate the taking of a cleek from the tee. The second shot may be described on a calm day as a longish pitch, and there is a big bunker in front of the green, rough ground and a sandy road behind, the railway to the right, and tenacious undergrowth to the left. There is apt to be an engine snorting loudly on the other side of the wall just as we are playing a critical and curly putt, and the said putt is none the easier from the engine having liberally besprinkled the green with cinders. Altogether, we shall have done good work if we get a four, and what a hole to do in three, when it is the thirty-seventh, as did Mr. John Ball in his great final with Mr. Tait—as good a hole under the circumstances that I ever saw played in my life.

GOLF COURSES

The second is quite one of the shortest of short holes on any first-class course, but it is not a bit easy, for a bunker behind the green has now been cut to reinforce the one in front, and the green is generally very keen.

The third is the 'Cardinal,' and has done a vast deal of mischief in its time. A topped brassey shot into the cavernous recesses of the bunker was generally thought to have cost Mr. Laidlay a championship when he played Mr. Peter Anderson; and, to come to more modern times, it was in this very same bunker that his supporters saw with horror the great Braid trying to throw away the championship in 1908 by playing a game of racquets against those ominous black boards. Yet, in the ordinary way, if we can but hit a reasonably straight tee-shot, we ought to send our second flying far over the Cardinal's sandy nob and a good long way on towards the green. Then comes a delicate little pitch over some hummocky ground, or, if we are lucky, a running-up shot, and we find ourselves on a small green under the shadow of the wall, and should obtain a respectable five; a four is, as a rule, the score of heroes only.

At the fourth we cross the wall with a drive that varies in direction with our bravery and skill. If we are very brave, and very skilful, we shall hit a ball with a suspicion of a slice that shall keep close to the rushing waters of the burn, and shall be rewarded with an easy pitch, and haply a putt for three. If we do not trust ourselves, we shall give the burn a wide berth and pull far away to the left, where we should still get a four—but only by means of a longer and harder approach shot.

The fifth is the 'Himalayas,' a hole of great fame, but no transcendent merit. A good cleek shot should see us safely over this big hill and on to the green on the other side, which is now guarded by pot-bunkers. All these holes at Prestwick seem to have some tragedy connected with them, and the 'Himalayas,' in all human probability, lost Mr. Hilton his third Open Championship in 1898. Just one bad shot—he can hardly have played another during the four rounds : but he made this one fatal mistake with a club that was strange to him (he has told the sad story himself), and took eight to the hole. Yet he finished in the end but two strokes behind the winner, Harry Vardon, and at one time he had actually caught him in this terrible stern chase.

After the 'Himalayas' come several holes which do not, like the earlier and later holes, cry aloud for description. The sixth has a sufficiently difficult second on to a plateau green, and there is fierce punishment for the slicer among the bents. The seventh is a long short hole (this is such a convenient expression that it must pass), with rushes to catch a slice; and of the eighth, which runs alongside the railway, I have already said something.

The ninth and tenth are really fine two-shot holes; as far as length is concerned, there are none better on the course, and they are both thoroughly difficult into the bargain. The green at the ninth is especially attractive and difficult, consisting of a little hilly peninsula of turf that

seems to jut out from a mainland of rough and bents. At
the tenth we sidle along parallel with the range of 'Himalayas,' and at the eleventh we cross them with a drive—
no cleek this time—for we have to carry as well the burn
that runs beyond them. Then we turn our noses for home
and make for the wall that we left behind us at the fourth
hole. We shall need two full shots, and then a little chip
on to a typical Prestwick green; long, narrow, and well
guarded by lumps and bumps of various shapes and sizes.
If, perchance, the wind is blowing very strongly behind
us, we may try to carry the wall in two, and the ball will
very likely light on the coping of the wall to bounce thence
into unfathomable bents, while we are left lamenting our
lack of contemptible prudence.

Now comes the 'Sea He'therick '—a charming hole with
a charming name, where the ball must be driven for the
distance of two very full shots along a sort of gully or
channel between the sand and bents on the right, and some
rough and hillocky country to the left. There is a narrow
little green, with odd corners and angles sticking out and
well guarded by hummocks, so that if we do get a four we
shall probably have to lay a singularly deft little pitch close
to the hole. A drive over the 'Goose-dubs' brings us to
a fairly ordinary fourteenth hole close to the club, and we
turn back to play the last four, the famous loop.

The chief characteristic of the fifteenth is that no two
persons are agreed on the best way of playing it. We may
lash out for death or glory with a driver, or play short with
the pusillanimous iron : we may go out to the right, or away

to the left, but wherever we try to go we shall heave a
sigh of relief if our ball finishes its agitating career upon
a piece of turf. Neither is the second an easy shot, for
the green is sloping and treacherous, and there are bunkers
to right and left. At the sixteenth—the 'Cardinal's Back'
—there is an insidious little pot-bunker in the middle of
the course, and we must drive either to the right or left
of it, or perhaps, wisest of all, aim straight at it in the
sure and certain hope of a sufficient measure of inaccuracy.

Now we come to the 'Alps,' one of the finest holes
anywhere, and *the* finest blind hole in all the world. The
drive must be hit straight and true down a valley between
two hills, and then comes the second, over a vast grassy
hill, beyond which we know that there is a bunker both
wide and deep. The ball may clear the hill and yet meet
with a dreadful fate, but there is glorious compensation in
the fact that if we do clear the chasm, we should be fairly
near the hole, and may possibly be putting for a
three. With no wind and a rubber-cored ball there
is nothing very tremendous in the achievement, but
nevertheless it is of the tremendous order of holes,
and it takes a stout-hearted man to get a four there at
all square and two to play. With a gutty ball it was
really a fine long, slashing carry, and to play short was
sometimes the better part of valour. Old Willy Park
wrecked his chances of yet another championship here in
1861, owing, to quote the appropriately solemn words of
the *Ayrshire Express*, to "a daring attempt to cross the
Alps in two, which brought his ball into one of the worst

GOLF COURSES

hazards of the green, and cost him three strokes—by no means the first time he has been seriously punished for similar avarice and temerity.'' It was in this bunker also that Mr. Tait played his ever-famous shot out of water, and Mr. Ball followed it with a superb niblick shot out of hard wet sand, which is not half as famous as it ought to be. Truly the 'Alps' is a hole with a great history.

After this the last hole is easy enough—a flat hole, just a little too long for the ordinary mortal to reach from the tee, save with a wind behind him. It can be reached, however, with a very fine shot, and I shall never forget the scene at the Open Championship in 1908, when Mr. Robert Andrew nearly holed it in one. It was in the qualifying competition, and Mr. Andrew, a strong local favourite and a truly magnificent player, had to do a two to equal Harry Vardon's record for the course of 72. He struck a gorgeous blow, and the ball sailed away straight as a die, and finished absolutely stone dead. With one wild yell of joy the crowd broke away from the tee, and raced down the slope for the green, even as the British square dashed down the hill after the flying French guard at Waterloo. It was at once a most thrilling and amusing spectacle.

So ends Prestwick; and what a jolly course it is, to be sure! What a jolly place to play, too, for we shall probably have had it reasonably to ourselves. It shares with Muirfield, among the great Scottish courses, the merit of being the private property of the club, and that is a merit that grows greater every year. It is a beautiful spot, moreover, and we may look at views of Arran and Ailsa Craig

PRESTWICK AND TROON

and the Heads of Ayr if we can allow our attention to wander so far from the game.

Tradition and romance cluster thickly around Prestwick, for it was here that old Tom Morris came in 1851—a little while after he and Allan Robertson had had a difference of opinion about Tom having played with the gutty ball. Here he stayed fourteen years before returning once and for all to his beloved St. Andrews, and it was here that the immortal Young Tom was born and first swung a precocious club. Prestwick was the home of the championship belt, which was competed for there every year from 1860 to 1870, when it passed into the permanent possession of Young Tom, who had won it three times running. If by some potent magic one could summon up the past at will, there is no golfing picture that I should like to see so much as that of Tommy's third win; 149 was his score for three rounds of the twelve-hole course, and he finished twelve strokes ahead of the two men who tied for second place. Whenever one is too much inclined to laud the golfers of the present to the detriment of those of the past, it is always a wholesome thing to remember that score of 149 round Prestwick. There must have been at least one very great golfer in those days.

The course at **Troon** is perhaps a little overshadowed by its more famous neighbour, but it is a very fine course nevertheless, especially since it has been lengthened of late years. It has, moreover, one of the finest short holes to be found anywhere. Here dwells Willy Fernie, and here it was that Braid and Herd went down so memorably before

211

GOLF COURSES

Vardon and Taylor in the great foursome over four greens. The Scottish pair left St. Andrews with a small advantage, but in Ayrshire a terrible thing befell them. Taylor and Vardon won so many holes—the number was well in double figures—that they came to the two English courses, St. Anne's and Deal, with a lead that nothing but a second miracle could take from them—and such miracles do not happen twice; it was surely one of the most extraordinary day's play in all the history of big matches. Troon, oddly enough, is one of the last places that one would expect such a collapse to occur. We know that when the greens are fast and fiery and not a little rough, a man who becomes afraid of his putter can lose an unlimited number of holes, but the greens at Troon are smooth and true, and of an almost velvety consistency that encourage us to putt above our form. They are certainly one of the features of the course.

Another pleasant feature of Troon is that the holes are known not simply by dull numbers, but each by its own name —'Dunure,' the 'Monk,' the 'Fox,' 'Sandhills'—they are good names; and what is more to the purpose, they are familiarly and habitually used, and not merely printed on the scoring cards. The first three holes run straight forward along a narrow strip of turf, having the seashore on the right-hand side; while at the third hole there is a small burn to be crossed. The fourth is 'Dunure,' a good two-shot hole, if the wind be not too strong against us, with big bunkers to right and left to catch the crooked tee-shot. 'Greenan' is the fifth—that takes its name from

212

TROON

The new short hole

PRESTWICK AND TROON

Greenan Castle on Carrick shore; and then comes one of the new holes, 'Turnberry' by name, in which the old 'Ailsa' is swallowed up. Here we need two full shots and a good iron to reach the green, which lies close to the Pow burn— the same burn that we have been trying to avoid on the links of Prestwick.

So far we have been going forward and hugging the shore, but now we turn inland to the left to play 'Tel-el-Kebir,' where is a narrow sloping green with a face in front of it. We may hope for our first three at the next, a short hole, that takes us back again towards the Pow burn; and then, turning inland once more, we come to the 'Monk,' with an exciting tee-shot over a big hill.

At Sandhills is another blind tee-shot over the sand dunes, followed by an accurate second into a green that lies close to the railway line. On the hill straight above the line is 'Sandhills,' the house from which the hole takes its name and the home of a family of many golfers, of whom one in particular, Mr. 'Nander' Robertson, is a very fine dashing player when he has a mind to it. The eleventh is a new hole, when we sidle along the railway; and then we drive out to sea once more at the 'Fox.' The covert which once gave this hole its name, has now been cut down, but it is good that the name should remain, though the foxes are gone. With a drive and a full iron we should reach the green here, but the prevailing wind blows off the sea, and may very easily elongate the iron into a cleek-shot. 'Burmah,' an ordinary four hole, and 'Alton,' which should be a three, give us a little breathing space before

213

GOLF COURSES

'Crosbie' and the 'Well,' which are both long holes, when we must rest content with fives—a thing which, in these days of long driving, we are a little apt to resent as a grievance. At the seventeenth one good full shot should take us on to a plateau green, tricky and difficult of access; the hole is called, somewhat singularly, the 'Rabbit,' but we must not be too hopeful of a low score in reliance of the cricketing significance of the word. A more or less commonplace four at the home hole brings a very good course to an end.

The turf is softer than that of Prestwick, and the ball runs but little after it pitches, so that, although Prestwick is possibly the longer by the chain measure, there is in the matter of playing length little difference between the two.

CHAPTER XIII.

IRELAND.

THERE is no country where the golfers are more keen or more hospitable than in Ireland, and the friendliness with which the inhabitants welcome their guests is only equalled by the earnestness with which they endeavour, and very often successfully, to beat them. It is a fine country for a golfing holiday, and this fact is now so thoroughly appreciated that Englishmen and Scotsmen pour over to the Irish courses every summer, and more especially to the particular course on which the Irish Championship is being played for. At this meeting may be had fierce golf, tempered by a proper measure of cheerfulness, on which those who have played in it—sad to say I am not one of them—are never weary of descanting. My own very delightful experience of Irish golf has come to me chiefly as one of two marauding bands, the English Bar and the Oxford and Cambridge Golfing Society, who periodically batten upon the hospitality of Dublin.

The chief Dublin courses are two—Dollymount and Portmarnock—though it would be unfair to omit some mention of Malahide—'the Island'—where there is golf to be had, which may legitimately be called sporting in the best sense of the word. Dollymount and Portmarnock are both also island courses in the sense that we have to cross the water to get to them. At Portmarnock this perilous feat is performed by car or boat, according as the tide is low or high; but at Dollymount there is a long causeway, and the worst possible sailor need not blench at the prospect.

I have a very great affection for **Dollymount.** I have played some very strenuous and delightful matches there, and, save possibly at St. Andrews, I feel as if I had been in more bunkers at Dollymount than on any other course. This seems to be *the* feature of Dollymount, the amount of low cunning, if I may so term it, with which the bunkers are placed. In writing that sentence I find that I have been guilty of a criminal pun without meaning it, because Mr. Barcroft, the secretary, is a great disciple of Mr. John Low in the matter of bunkering. He has saturated his mind in that most charming and instructive of books, *Concerning Golf,* and then he has gone forth valiantly with his shovel. The result is that there are many pitfalls, which are worthy of Mr. Low's definition of what a bunker should be. ''Bunkers, if they be good bunkers and bunkers of strong character, refuse to be disregarded, and insist on asserting themselves; they do not mind being avoided, but they decline to be ignored.' There are some fine, towering hills at Dollymount, but it is not these that make the player's knees to knock together; it is the little

216

DOLLYMOUNT

The first tee, looking towards Howth

IRELAND

pots of innocuous aspect that most emphatically decline to be ignored.

A first glance at the course produces much the same effect on the mind as does Hoylake. It looks a little flat, and bare, and even dull; we do not see where the holes are and whence and whither the players are going and what they are trying to do. As at Hoylake, the first impression is utterly wrong, as we soon discover when we begin to play, more especially if we have been maltreated by the Irish Channel on the previous evening. The first thing that strikes us is that we ought to be beginning with a nice symmetrical row of fours, and that ugly disfiguring fives will insist on creeping in. At the first we really ought to do a four, but still there are a variety of things to prevent such a consummation : a pot-bunker to catch a pulled tee-shot, a bunker in the right-hand side of the green, and a considerable possibility of taking three putts on a green which is as good as it is usually fast and difficult. At the second the trouble is of a bolder and, in a sense, a more commonplace character, a large and ravenous bunker, which must be carried with a good second shot, and then turning back towards the club again we play a hole where almost meticulous accuracy is necessary if we are to get the perfect four, wherein the fourth shot consists of our opponent saying, contrary to the recommendations of the Rules of Golf Committee, ''That will do.'' Crooked driving may be definitely punished by pot-bunkers, or, if we are lucky, it may only entail the most difficult of approach shots, in which we may have to try a pitch of

217

really desperate difficulty over flanking bunkers. Only if we drive with absolute accuracy we shall be properly rewarded by being able to play a pitch and run shot straight —or let us hope so at least—up to the flag.

There is to be no pitching or running at the fourth— not at any rate with the second shot—but a fine, high carrying stroke with a wooden club to take us home on to a green that lies well protected by hollows and hummocks; a really good four this time, and we must do a man's work to get it. These first four holes always run together in my mind partly because of their uniform excellence and partly because we now branch off into somewhat different country, a country of bents and big sandhills. The fifth is chiefly notable for what I may call a typical Sandwich shot from the tee, and then comes a region that I know only by sight, for there have lately been some new holes made there. It is a region of rolling dunes and bristling bents; I am told the new holes are long and difficult, with narrow and exacting greens, and knowing the country and Mr. Barcroft I can well believe it.

Of the other holes on the way out I must spare a special word for the eighth—it was old seventh—one of the very best 'round-the-corner' holes that I know. The whole face of nature bids us slice from the tee, and the wind generally encourages us to do so, and yet we must pull resolutely out to the left in order to open up the way for our approach shot on to a green that nestles among the hills. If we fail to pull, or if we are tempted to use the wind too freely, we may have a very long drive on which to plume ourselves, but shall have an impossible second, and we shall take five to the hole.

It seems to me that the first few holes on the way home are not so good as the outgoing ones, save that there is a fine tee-shot to be played at thirteen, between the marsh on the one side and a series of pot-bunkers on the other. The sixteenth, however, is good, with the green lying in a long, narrow hollow; and the seventeenth is really very good indeed. It is long and narrow and all the more frightening because there is hardly anything in the way on the straight line to the hole. There are bunkers at the side, however, and more alarming still is the fact that we are always playing along a hog's back, with marsh to the right and rough to the left. Finally, there is a green not very fiercely guarded, but full of terribly difficult curves and angles, wherein the holing of the very shortest putt is a matter for much prayerful 'borrowing.' I cannot help regretting the old eighteenth, which has now disappeared. That tee-shot, with the chance of breaking a club-house window, tempted one very strongly to the taking of a cleek, and that is a testimonial in itself. However, on high days and holidays the general public congregated there so freely that the death of one of them was probably only a matter of time, and so the hole had to go. The old seventeenth now promoted to being the home hole is a very fine hole if there is much adverse wind, for then there is a fine long second to be played over the corner of a territory, which is out of bounds, and those shots in which the ball has to leave the limits of the course for part of its career are never pleasant, when it comes to a pinch.

The last few holes are all quite sufficiently unpleasant, when the struggle is a keen one; worst of all, of course, when a lead that once seemed thoroughly satisfactory is fast vanishing away. I have vivid recollections of two such matches—one with Mr. Cairnes and one with Mr. Lionel Munn—and I can still very well remember two odious, curly, short putts on the seventeenth green—it was the sixteenth then. Heaven be praised! the ball on both occasions trickled in somehow, but I still shudder at the recollection.

I also feel just a little uncomfortable at the thought of the last occasion on which I crossed over from Portmarnock to the mainland. When the tide is low, one can drive across an expanse of soft, wet sand while clinging ungracefully but tenaciously to an outside car, but on this occasion the tide was not low, and we had to make the journey by sailing boat. A snowstorm was raging intermittently, and the wind blew piercing, cold and strong, reminding one with its every blast that on the morrow all the horrors of the Irish Channel had to be faced. On such a day the causeway at Dollymount is infinitely preferable; but, on the other hand, when the weather is pleasant, the necessity for this crossing in miniature gives to Portmarnock a fascination of its own. There is an element of romance in playing golf even on a temporarily sea-girt island.

Perhaps the outstanding beauty of **Portmarnock** lies in its putting greens. They are good and true, which is a

PORTMARNOCK (1)

The second shot at the eighteenth hole

merit given to many greens, and they are very fast without being untrue, which is given only to a few, and is a rare and shining virtue. For a worse than indifferent putter to praise keen greens shows him to be a nobly impartial critic, for there is nothing that finds out so quickly the bad putter, that sifts so surely the wheat from the chaff. Most of us fare passably well as long as we are on a slow and velvety lawn, but with increased keenness comes an enormously increased difficulty in hitting freely and firmly —those two cardinal points of putting skill—and behold! we are entirely undone.

I have never seen the Portmarnock greens when they are presumably at their keenest, namely, in hot, dry, summer weather, but even on a raw day at Easter time they demand that the ball should be soothed rather than hit towards the hole. I have read somewhere a story of a famous Scottish professional who declared that on his first visit to the course he arrived on the first green in two perfect shots, and had ultimately to hole a four-yard putt for a seven.

To praise the greens too vehemently is very often to cast an undeserved slur on the rest of the course; it is rather like saying of a man "He is a good short-game player," for then one is always understood to mean that in regard to his driving he is one of the great family of scufflers. I therefore make all haste to say that Portmarnock does not live by greens alone. Far from it: it is a good, long, bold course, with plenty of natural features, and, moreover, it has of late years been considerably lengthened and otherwise altered for the better. Before the alterations the golf was not, I say it with fear and trembling, particularly difficult. So long as a man played with a reasonable degree of accuracy and did not lose himself on the greens, he might expect to do quite a good score. Now, however, the course has been 'bolstered up,' if I may say so, in its weakest parts, and in the region of the sixth and seventh holes the golf is much longer and more difficult than it used to be.

It is rather characteristic of Portmarnock that at some of the best holes the player's course lies along the bottom of gullies that wind their way between hills on either side. Of such is the fourth hole—a really fine hole—where the gully bends as it goes, so that there is plenty to be gained by hugging the left-hand side with a judicious but not a doting affection. The hole is of a good length, needing at least two shots, and possibly infinitely more, for on both sides of the little gully are sandy slopes well covered with tenacious bents. Before, however, we get to the fourth there is a very distinctly good tee-shot to be played to the third along a strath of turf that stretches, narrow and hog's-backed, between hills on the one side and bare sand upon the other.

The fifth, again, has a fine tee-shot over a big bunker, which should see us safely at the bottom of another gorge between the hills, with a good second shot to follow. Then follow some of the newer holes amid a broken country of smaller undulations, and then we come back to the club-house again for the ninth. The tenth has a very interesting

PORTMARNOCK (2)

Coming home

and difficult second on to a green that lies in a little nook or angle guarded by a turf wall; and the twelfth is a short hole that may be deserving of criticism, but appeals to the affections of many. Need I add that the shot is a blind one, but it is a fascinating pitch, nevertheless, into a crater green with its concomitant admixture of hopes and fears. After this the golf, though good, is for a while less attractive. The land is flatter, and though the holes are long, there is just that depressing suggestion of an agricultural character such as we have in some of the holes beyond the wall at Prestwick. The course ends splendidly, however, with a really fine hole, its green narrow, well guarded, and difficult to stay upon. The turf throughout is a joy alike to walk or play on, and altogether Portmarnock is a place to leave with a very genuine regret, even in a snowstorm.

On leaving Dublin we may betake ourselves southward to the very charming course of **Lahinch** in County Clare, where, if the holes are rather unduly blind and put a great premium on local knowledge, the golf is yet intensely enjoyable. The greatest compliment I have heard paid to Lahinch came from a very fine amateur golfer, who told me that it might not be the best golf in the world, but was the golf he liked best to play. Lest this may be attributed to patriotic prejudice, I may add that he was an Englishman born and bred. Delightful though Lahinch is, however, it is rather to the north that we must go to get a variety of good courses. In Donegal there is Buncrana, on Lough Swilly, a really good nine-hole course

GOLF COURSES

which has nurtured the best player than has yet come out of Ireland, Mr. Lionel Munn: there is also Rosapenna, and there is Portsalon, which lies at the far end of the lough, a truly lovely spot, with a thoroughly entertaining golf course. I must put in one word for the quaintest and most charming little nine-hole course at Macamish, also on the shores of Lough Swilly, which can be reached by sailing across from Buncrana or by driving from anywhere else an interminable number of Irish miles over a rocky make-shift of a road. It is the most purely amateur course in the world, and also, if more than two or three are gathered together upon it, the most perilous. The holes cross and recross each other and everybody aims at his own particular hole in a light-hearted, pic-nicking frame of mind, and perfectly regardless of the lives of others. For pure, unadulterated fun I have yet to see the equal of this course.

However, we must leave the frivolities of Macamish and betake ourselves for some serious golf to Portrush, in County Antrim. **Portrush** has many claims to fame, and amongst others is that of having produced a wonderful race of lady golfers. Considering how keen they are, and how good are the courses on which they play, the men of Ireland, albeit there have been some fine players amongst them, have not so far particularly distinguished themselves, but as regards ladies' golf, Ireland was for a time supreme. Miss Rhona Adair and Miss May Hezlet (they are both married now, but the old names sound the more familiar) used to win the championship one after the other

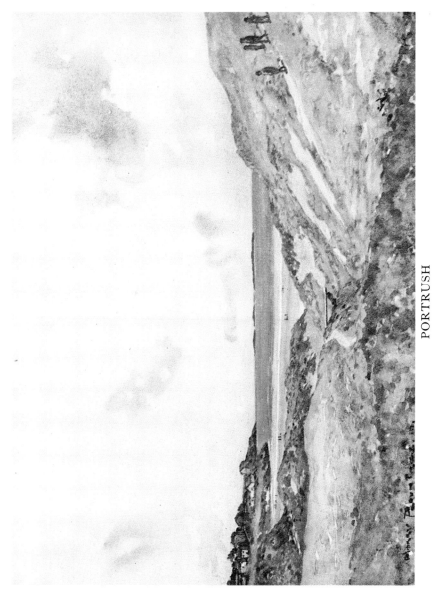

PORTRUSH

Coming to the seventeenth green

with monotonous regularity, and close on their heels flocked further and innumerable members of the Hezlet family.

Whether there are any subtle qualities about the course which naturally tend to the development of female champions I cannot say; I at least have not discovered them. At any rate it is a very delightful place in which to play golf, for persons of either sex. The air is so fine that the temptation to play three rounds is very hard to overcome, while I may quote, solely on the authority of a friend, this further testimonial to it, that it has the unique property of enabling one to drink a bottle of champagne every night and feel the better for it.

Portrush stands on a rocky promontory that juts out into the Atlantic, and, if I may allude to such trivialities, the scenery of the coast is wonderfully striking. On the east are the White Rocks, tall limestone cliffs that lead to Dunluce Castle and the headlands of the Giant's Causeway. On the west are the hills of Inishowen, beyond which lie Portsalon and Buncrana and the links of Donegal. It is, however, a remarkable thing that though golf courses are often in lovely places it frequently so happens that the beauties of the landscape are to be seen from anywhere except the course. Who, for instance, ever heard of a self-respecting sea-side course where one could get a view of the sea! One may hear it perhaps roaring or murmuring, according to its mood, beyond an interminable row of sandhills, but save with the artificial aid of a high tee one never dreams of seeing it. So it is at Portrush, in accordance with the best traditions, and only two or

P
225

three times in the course of the round does a view of the surrounding beauties threaten our mental concentration on the matter in hand.

Again, according to the most approved Scottish traditions the course begins, as one may say, in the middle of the town. Thence during its outward journey it skirts the sandhills on the landward side, and one or two of the holes are just a little inland in character and not particularly entertaining. The homeward journey is, on the whole, the more fascinating, and from the eleventh hole onwards there are a succession of hills and valleys of a truly heroic character. If, however, there are one or two dullish holes on the way out, the course begins splendidly with as good a two-shot hole as can well be; too good a hole almost to play so early before the match has had time to develop. A ridge running diagonally and away towards the left calls for a fine tee-shot if it is to be cleared in the straight line, while a sandy hill covers half the green on the right-hand side, and repays the man who has hit a good tee-shot by punishing his opponent who has not. This first used to be followed by another equally good, if not better, two-shot hole, but the old second and third have, as before mentioned, now been run into one, and there are many who say that one more has been added to that long list of crimes which have been committed through the desire for length. The fifth is another good hole on the way out—two reasonable shots for a reasonable hitter to a green that lies just on the top of a high, swelling slope : one of those holes where for some inscrutable reason it is very easy to be either too far or too short, and very difficult to hit off the distance exactly.

Thence I will make so bold as to skip to the big hills and dales of the last few holes, which are cast, as I have said, in a distinctly heroic mould. There is the thirteenth, which is a fine one-shot hole, although it is a blind; the fourteenth, the famous 'Long Valley,' which was once knee-deep in soft moss, and is now as hard as St. Andrews in the middle of a hot, dry August; and the fifteenth and sixteenth, where in each case a real straight, well-hit drive reaps its due reward.

All these are excellent, but a tear may legitimately be shed over the old seventeenth, which, like the old second, had to disappear through the desire for length and the subsequent reconstruction. This old seventeenth was a splendid one-shot hole, for with this one shot the ball had to be struck over one of the hugest of bunkers on to a green of saucer shape. So alarming was this bunker that it is recorded that two gentlemen of oriental origin, who were playing a match for a stake of ten pounds, were simultaneously smitten with terror and remorse when they saw it, that, although the match stood all square at the time, so they resolved to reduce the wager to the sum of one shilling. It was surely wrong to do away with a hole that could produce a result so wholly admirable.

Another very beautiful place with a very delightful course is **Newcastle** in County Down. Newcastle has lately been altered and extended, and has consequently risen to a position of greater dignity among golf courses. It was always looked upon with great affection by all who knew it, but this was a love a little akin to that which the frequenters of Burnham used to feel for the many high hills and blind holes of the Somersetshire course. Everybody liked Newcastle, but they spoke of it as "'a wonderful natural course," or "the best fun in the world"—expressions which rather begged the question as to its exact golfing merits. That is all changed, however, and to-day Newcastle is as long as anyone can desire: indeed, in places almost too long. I remember meeting a very distinguished player on his return from Newcastle soon after the alterations had been made, when there was still practically no run in the new ground, and he solemnly averred that he had never played so many brassey shots in all his life.

The course lies among the sandhills under the shadow of Slieve Donard, the tallest of the Mourne Mountains, and so close to the sea that we may reach the shore with our first tee-shot. No amount of reconstruction has done away with the original character of the course; we still have many big carries to compass with the tee-shot, and a good deal more pitching than running to do with our iron clubs. However, we must not run away with the idea that we shall have done all that is demanded of us when we have hit a ball hard and high over a hill somewhere or other into the distance. Trouble lurks at the sides as well as in the centre of the fairway, and for all the boldness and bigness of the hazards it is really a straight rather than a long driver's course. The greens are good, and some-

NEWCASTLE

The ninth carry and the club-house

times inclined to be slow; they lie, moreover, in a good many instances, in those pleasing little hollows which are the most adroit flatterers in the whole world of golf. The turf on the outward journey is of the ideal sea-side kind, but on the way home we fancy that we detect something more of an inland character about it.

Flitting, like arbitrary bees, from one hole to another, we must pause a moment over the first, which is one of the best of the long holes, and has an admirable tee-shot. So has the second, while there is an approach shot of much interest and delicacy to be played at the third. The sixth again is a memorable hole, of no great length, but considerable difficulty. We need but one shot to go from the tee to the high plateau green where the hole is, but the sides of the plateau fall very quickly away, and there must be plenty of stop on the ball or it will inevitably overrun its mark.

On the way home, again, there is another arresting hole, the sixteenth. We mount a high tee on one side of an enormous bunker, and must hit a sheer carry of goodness knows how many yards on to a green also perched high in the air upon the further side. It is a distinctly heroic hole; and the seventeenth and eighteenth, in trying to live up to its standard, have grown so long as to be just a little bit dull. They are, however, I believe, to be lopped and pruned of their superfluous yards, and should then make a fine finish. It should be added for those who like to play their golf in comfort, that the first tee, the tenth tee,

GOLF COURSES

the club-house and the hotel lie, all four of them, close together; not that Newcastle really needs these adventitious advantages, for it is one of the very pleasantest places for golf in all Ireland.

CHAPTER XIV.

WALES.

THERE are several very excellent courses in Wales, but I am quite determined to put Aberdovey first—not that I make for it any claim that it is the best, not even on the strength of its alphabetical pre-eminence, but because it is the course that my soul loves best of all the courses in the world. Every golfer has a course for which he feels some such blind and unreasoning affection. When he is going to this his golfing home he packs up his clubs with a peculiar delight and care; he anxiously counts the diminishing number of stations that divide him from it, and finally steps out on the platform, as excited as a schoolboy home for the holidays, to be claimed by his own familiar caddie. A golfer can only have one course towards which he feels quite in this way, and my one is **Aberdovey**.

I can just faintly remember the beginning of golf at Aberdovey in the early eighties. Already rival legends have clustered round that beginning, but the true legend says that the founder was Colonel Ruck, who, having played some golf at Formby, borrowed nine flower pots from a

231

lady in the village and cut nine holes on the marsh to put them in. The first five holes as the visitor knows them now were then but a wilderness. There was no ' Cader ' and no ' Pulpit'; we had a long weary walk along the road to the level-crossing, and began with the present sixth hole, which was then guarded by a fine clump of gorse, long since cut to pieces by merciless niblicks. Then came a period when we began and ended on the piece of land which now serves Aberdovey as a cricket ground, and there was a wonderful last hole in which we drove off from the present eighteenth tee, carried with our second shot the railway line and a mighty pile of sleepers, and holed out on the present cricket pitch. Finally, at the time of the first meeting at Easter, 1893, the course had taken something like the shape which it has kept ever since, save for the quite recent introduction of the new home-coming holes. I have in a dusty old album a group taken at that first meeting by a local photographer. I cannot count more than ten players, nor do I believe that there were any more. They stand ranged with their caddies in front of a bunker and a turf wall most curiously and artistically castellated, while behind is a motley gathering of local spectators arrayed in bowler hats. That humble little meeting, with its ten players, was considered a vast success, though I cannot think that the play was very good, since I remember winning the scratch medal with 100, and the best actual score returned during the three days was but three strokes lower. Aberdovey has made great strides since those days. The golf is very good, and will soon,

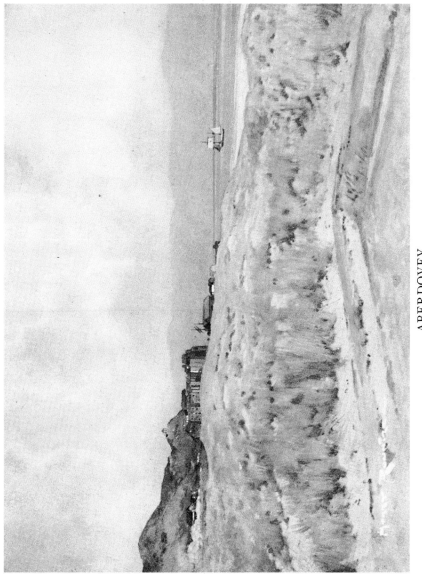

ABERDOVEY

The village from the second tee

WALES

I suppose, be made better, although, if one only loves a course well enough, even the most obvious improvement feels to be almost a desecration. Moreover, the place has a charm which brings the same people back to it year after year with a wonderful constancy of affection.

Aberdovey stands at the mouth of the Dovey Estuary, and the links are on a long, narrow strip of turf stretching between the sandhills and the shore on the one side, and a range of hills on the other. The sandhills are many and imposing, but nature has not disposed them with a very kindly hand. There is no turf on the far side of them— nothing but the shore and the waves—and so, although they make a most effective series of lateral bunkers, it is not possible to dodge in and out amongst them in quite the same fascinating way as at Prestwick or Sandwich. Moreover, till quite lately we could not use them at all in the home-coming nine holes, owing to the difficulty of properly draining some of the marshy ground at their foot. That difficulty has now, however, been done away with, at least as regards the summer, and there are some fine new holes, still a little rough, but improving rapidly, where we have to play with something more than ordinary accuracy between a never-ending range of hills on the right, and thick, unyielding clumps of rushes on the left.

As I said before, the course lies on a long narrow strip of golfing country, with the result that the holes have to go straight out and home again, and we have often either to struggle all the way out against the wind, and then be blown homewards, or *vice versa*. This is, of course, a disadvantage, since the holes in one direction are apt to become too long, and those in the other too short. I remember that on one occasion there was a Bogey competition, and a terribly strong wind, which blew dead ahead all the way out; it blew so hard that no human creature could hope to reach any of the first nine greens in anything like the right number of shots, and I believe the man who ultimately won the competition was eight down to Bogey at the turn.

There is probably no course that has its first tee so near the station. We tee up within the shortest possible stone's throw of the platform, and drive over a waste of sand and stones, that is still fairly formidable, though neither so sandy or so stony as it was in the days when it served as an impromptu football ground for the villagers. A good drive lands us in a country of those grassy hummocks, which are a conspicuous feature of the course, and a firm iron shot over a bunker should get us a four. The pitch, however, has to be an accurate one, and this applies to the approaching throughout, since the greens are decidedly small and there is no great chance of recovering by a very long putt laid dead. To do a low score at Aberdovey a man must either be keeping his iron shots ruled rigidly on the pin, or he must lay a number of little chip shots from off the edge of the green within holing distance; this, moreover, is not a particularly easy thing to do, since the greens are full of natural dells and hillocks. The second and third holes have very similar tee-shots; there are several small sandhills to carry, and severe punishment for a pulled shot. The approach to the third hole is a particularly attractive one, since the green is almost entirely circled round with small hills, and there is only a very narrow opening through which to play; against the wind the ball may be pitched up boldly enough, but down wind there is nothing for it but a running shot, and that a very accurate one.

The fourth hole is known to all Aberdoveyites as 'Cader,' and is as good a specimen of the blind short hole as is to be found. There is a big hill in front of the tee, shored up with black timbers, and the green has the transcendent merit for this type of hole that it is not too big. There is no vast meadow of turf to play on to, like the Maiden green at Sandwich, and the ball has to do something more than carry the hill-top. Cader used to be particularly memorable a few years back, when the small caddies, stationed on the top to watch the fate of the ball, used to cry out ''On the green,'' with a curiously melancholy, piping note. Now alas! they have become more sophisticated, and merely signal with the hand in the orthodox manner. It is but a poor exchange, and we sadly miss the old familiar cry.

After Cader we must take a short walk along a winding path among the hills which takes us on to the 'Pulpit' tee, where we stand high above all the world, with the sea on our left and the whole course stretching away before us in the distance. The tee-shot is by no means one of the most difficult, but certainly one of the pleasantest that I know, and gives a full measure of sensual delight. Then we must leave the hills for a while and strike inland to play some flatter holes that wind their way by the side of the railway. The sixth and seventh are both very fine two-shot holes, and then at the long eighth we meet with a characteristic Aberdovey hazard, familiarly and affectionately known as the 'leeks.' They are in fact irises, but they have always been the 'leeks' since Peter Paxton christened them so, under the impression that the national emblem must naturally be found upon a Welsh course. Paxton is not the only man who has found sad trouble in the leeks, for they are wonderfully thick and retentive, and the wise man pulls very wide away to the left at the eighth and ninth, and does not try to run things at all fine.

So far we have gone practically straight ahead, but at the tenth we turn sharply to the left and prepare for our homeward journey. This tenth is a truly beautiful short hole : in length about a cleek or long iron shot on a still day, with a really horrible bunker, long, deep, and wide, stretching before the green and throwing out a sandy tentacle far to the right to catch a long sliced shot. It is really a better hole than Cader, in that we can see far more clearly where we are going, and, when the wind is against us and we must needs take a wooden club, there is no finer one-shot hole in the world.

Now we come to the parting of the ways, where the new holes break away to the right towards the sandhills, and the old holes are on the flat ground, over which we journeyed outwards. There is among the old holes a beautiful thirteenth, with a narrow little green beset on

every side, so that the tee-shot had to be accurate in order
to make the second possible. That hole we shall miss
sadly, but otherwise the new holes are far the better : long
raking holes between hills and rushes that give the course
just the extra touch of length and difficulty that it wanted.
We emerge on to the old ground again to play the 'Crater,'
a hole that we are fond of for old sake's sake, though it is in
reality a bad and fluky one, as 'punchbowl' holes generally
are. The sixteenth, however, is a really good one, with
a horribly narrow tee-shot between the railway on the left
and a wilderness of sandhills on the right; it is capable of
ruining any score, and no man is a medal winner till he
has played that shot—with a cleek, if he is prudent—and
sees the ball lying safely on the turf. The seventeenth
has a fine tee-shot from one of the spurs of Cader and
another punchbowl green, which follows all too soon after
the fifteenth, and then we finish with a fine, long, free-
hitting hole over clumps of rushes.

Thus ends the course, and I know it so well that I find
it very hard to criticize or appraise at its just worth. One
thing may safely be said, that it provides a fine school for
iron club shots, whether short or long. There are a great
many holes—perhaps too many—which need a long iron
shot for the second, and these shots have to be played from
every variety of stance and lie on to greens that are good,
but uniformly small. There is, too, no better course for
teaching the little chip or run up, play it how you will,
from the confines of the green—the shot which professionals
play so wonderfully well, and many amateurs play so badly.

GOLF COURSES

The tee-shots are good, without being very remarkable, and there is perhaps a lack of full brassey shots to be lashed right up to the hole; that, however, is a criticism to which, in these days of mighty hitting and rubber-cored balls, many courses are open. Yet when the wind is adverse, and the iron shots become wooden club shots, the comparative smallness of the greens makes them wooden club shots of the very best, and I ask for nothing pleasanter to look back upon than a string of fours going out against a wind at Aberdovey.

I have tried as a rule to avoid invidious comparisons between course and course, but it may be pardonable to make a short and wholly friendly comparison between Aberdovey and Harlech, because, although near neighbours, they have such very different characteristics. At Aberdovey the holes go straight out and home again; at Harlech they tack backwards and forwards, this way and that. In the same way the Aberdovey sandhills run in one unbroken line, while at Harlech they are more scattered, and can therefore be used in more different ways. Aberdovey is a course of small, undulating greens, while Harlech has larger and flatter ones. Finally, the charms of Aberdovey grow on one slowly, but also, I think, surely, while Harlech fascinates at the first glance.

Small wonder if the visitor falls in love with **Harlech at** first sight, for no golf course in the world has a more splendid background than the old castle, which stands at the top of a sheer precipice of rock looking down over the links. Wherever we go it is never out of sight, and though

238

HARLECH

Looking across the fourth hole

we may glance away at the hills with Snowdon in the distance, we always come back to the castle with a never-satisfied longing. It is so obviously splendid that we might imagine that we should in time grow tired of it, but we never do.

The holes at Harlech that have always left the most vivid impression on my mind, perhaps because, owing to the rather leisurely Cambrian trains, I have not been there half as often as I should like, are those at the beginning and end of the course. Those in the middle, possibly because they have been altered at times or because they are not so markedly characteristic, are more blurred in the memory. Yet it is, I hasten to add, that all the golf is good, very good indeed, and fit to test the very best of players.

At the first hole there is a kind of ditch and bank to carry, a little severe when the player is stiff and ill at ease with his clubs, and a particularly excellent green. Then we turn almost directly back and get rather nearer to the first of those stone walls, which are so common an object in the landscape in North Wales, and quite one of the distinctive features of Harlech. At the third we are fighting with stone walls all the way, and a most effective hazard they make. This third is a really fine hole, for there is a whole stroke to be gained by a drive that is long and bold and clings as near to the wall as safety permits. The first shot has to be played parallel to the wall, or rather to two neighbouring walls, between which lies a sandy cart track full of unspeakable ruts. Then at the second we have to make up our minds whether or not to go for the green, which lies beyond the two walls, and is further guarded by yet a third wall, which runs at right angles to the other two. If we have not gone far enough, or if we have kept too much to the left, there is nothing for it but to play another shot straight along, and so home with a pitch for our third. If, however, we have driven far and sure, we may take the brassey, carrying all three walls at one fell swoop, and accomplish a four. Moreover, it is a four that is a real joy to do. It is none of your 'Bogey fours,' for the miserable old gentleman would never attempt that dashing second, but would proceed pawkily and by stages, pitching on to the green with his third, and getting a commonplace and respectable five. Thereby he will often win the hole from us who have died a glorious death in the sandy road, but at least we shall have tried to quit ourselves like men.

The fourth is a one-shot hole, which likewise calls for hard hitting. It is never short, and against the wind a really big shot is needed to carry the bunker, which is made the taller and more frightening by a timbered face. The green is flat and easy, and if we can reach it there should be no excuse for more than two putts.

The holes that come after this have undergone a good many alterations at different times. They are good sound golf every one of them, but it is when we turn our faces homeward toward the castle, and are approaching the almost equally famous 'Castle' bunker, that Harlech becomes most memorable.

240

WALES

At this fourteenth, if we are fighting a fierce match, we feel that the crucial time is coming, for we are now going to plunge into the heart of the hills for five eminently critical and exciting holes. The first of them entails a shot over the 'Castle' bunker, and never was a bunker that more thoroughly belied its true character by a mild and harmless exterior. All that we see in front of us is a grassy bank, with a guiding flag fluttering on the top; and, ignorance being here most emphatically bliss, we may hit a fine shot as straight as an arrow and be congratulated on reaching the green. It is only when we have climbed to the top of that innocent-looking bank that we shall see what we have escaped, a perfect Sahara of sand that stretches nearly to the edge of the green. This green, too, is guarded by a series of knolls and hummocks—there are perhaps rather too many of them—and we may have been very nearly straight and yet be confronted with an extremely awkward little pitch. The hole is a terribly blind one : rather too blind to be classed among the greatest of one-shot holes, but it is impossible not to be swayed by our emotions rather than by pure reason, and our emotions tell us that it is a glorious hole.

There is another hill to carry at the fifteenth, while the sixteenth has a green of almost infinite possibilities in the matter of tortuous and tricky putts. There is nothing tricky about the seventeenth, however—nothing but straight, honest hitting, and the chance of a clean stroke to be gained by it. The green lies in a hollow at the foot of the hills, and in front of it is a bunker and a most uncompromising stone wall. Two really fine shots will carry the wall; let the tee-shot be a little less than good and we must needs play short and be content with a five: that is the entire story of the hole, and a very fine seventeenth hole it is. The eighteenth is mild by comparison, but a good straight tee-shot is needed to reach the green, which is well guarded by pot-bunkers.

Harlech is rich in the possession of one of the best secretaries in the world, Mr. More, and also in one of the most popular of handicap competitions, the Harlech Town Bowl. The fields that enter for this tournament every August are really enormous, and to win it is no mean feat. In this same tournament Mr. Hilton, when he was at his very best, played some of the most extraordinary golf of his life. I am almost afraid to say how heavily he was penalized, but I am nearly sure that he owed eight. I know that in one round he had to give a third to Mr. Palmer, who, if not quite as good as he is now, was at any rate a very good player, and, what is more, played well in this particular match. However, Mr. Hilton beat him after a great struggle, fought his way into the final, and there trampled on an unfortunate and probably awe-stricken adversary. He was laying his brassey shots within a few feet of the hole, and generally making light of difficulties which any visitor to Harlech will find are not to be treated lightly.

To get from North to South Wales is not so easy a matter as might be supposed. It entails much waiting at junctions, which have been placed in some of the most

WALES

melancholy and deserted spots on the face of the earth. However, once arrived in South Wales, there is plenty of golf to be had, some of it very good. There is a very fine course near Llanelly, Ashburnham by name, which, alas! I have never seen; and there is Southerndown, in Glamorganshire, which is growing fast into fame. Near Cardiff there is Radyr and Penarth, the latter having a truly glorious view over the British Channel, but being sometimes afflicted with muddiness. Then, also in Glamorgan, there are the very excellent links of Porthcawl.

Links they may worthily be called, for the golf at **Porthcawl** is the genuine thing—the sea in sight all the time, and the most noble bunkers. True to its national character, the course also boasts of stone walls. Of my visits to Porthcawl I retain two particularly vivid recollections. The first is of a hole that has long since disappeared, since that part of the ground is no more played over. As I remember it, it was by far the longest hole in the world, Blackheath not excepted. Perhaps it has become stretched in my memory, or possibly the reason is that I played the hole against a most prodigious driver, Mr. Edmund Spencer, who was one of the hopes of Hoylake in these days, but has now most reprehensibly given up the game. I do not think there were many hazards in the way; one was simply told to aim at a white rock in the dim distance, and to keep on hitting till one got there. To make matters worse, it was the very first hole, so that one was nearly prostrate before the round had really begun.

My other recollections of a more cheerful nature is of a

243

hole which was far easier to get into than any other hole in the world. The hole was not in itself by any means a simple one, involving a struggle with a stone wall and a long shot up a hill, but the green-keeper had selected a delightful spot for the hole at the bottom of a hollow with shelving sides. Once arrived within approaching distance of the hole, one had only to play the ball some few yards beyond the hole and it would topple gently back, not merely to lie stone dead, but actually to go in. The Welsh Championship meeting was going on at the time, and all sorts of wonders were recorded. One competitor holed a full brassey shot, and threes were as common as black-berries. The putting was becoming almost farcical, when one day there came a day of reckoning. I remember being left with a putt of some eight or ten yards, and, banging the ball past the hole with a light and careless heart, fully prepared to see it come trickling in. Alas! the green was a little wet that morning, and the ball stuck firmly on the opposite slope and refused to come back. I can still see that ball perched upon the bank and grinning at me. "Sold again" it was obviously and impudently saying.

At Porthcawl, as it is now, there are some very good holes. Of the two-shot holes, the fourth is excellent, and has a formidable second shot over a big and boarded bunker. The sixth is very similar, both as regards quality and quantity. Then there is the eleventh, where a really long, raking second over a big bunker should entail a four, and the utter destruction of Bogey and other cautious

PORTHCAWL

Going to the eighteenth green

players who duly play short with their second shots. Another good one is the ninth, with a long carry up a hill on to a crater green—a green which I suspect of having been the scene of the putting exploits that I have narrated, though my memory is a little vague on this point.

Of the single-shot holes there is a fine long carry—the shot has to be practically all carry—on to the third green. The sixteenth is another that is good, and the course ends with an exceedingly difficult single-shot hole. There is in the minds of many a prejudice against finishing with a short hole, and it is certainly an ending which is not to be found on many good courses. Nevertheless, if the shot be only difficult enough, it is a little hard to see why a short hole should not make a really fine finish. There is an unpleasant feeling of finality about the tee-shot at any short hole, which never allows us to feel wholly comfortable, and certainly ' Hades ' or the ' Maiden ' would be infinitely more alarming if they came at the end of the round instead of in the earlier part of the round, when no mistake is irreparable. From the spectator's point of view, it is desirable to get the player to the eighteenth tee in the last state of nervous exhaustion, and a tricky, difficult one-shot hole accomplishes that rather inhuman purpose to perfection.

Not far from Porthcawl—as the aeroplane flies—is another excellent course, Southerndown. It is perched high aloft and looks down on Porthcawl, amid the many other glories of a beautiful view. You may look out far over the sea, or again over a wide stretch of the best kind of English—or rather Welsh—landscape. The breezes blow cool and fresh here, and on a still and stifling August day, when the golfer is almost too limp to crawl round Porthcawl, he will be wise to refresh himself by a round on the heights of **Southerndown.**

In one way the course is rather singular. Being high in the air and not down on the level of the shore, it has many of the characteristics of the typical downland courses. It has their big rolling slopes and deep gullies, but it has not, curiously to relate, the typical down turf. The winds of centuries have blown so much sand up from the seashore that they have practically succeeded in imbuing the turf of the downs with a second sandy nature. The sand does not go very deep down; indeed, if you dig far down you come to uncompromising rock; but this, so to speak, veneer of sand has a great deal to do with making the course the good and pleasing one that it is. An example of this blowing of the sand is to be seen in a huge sandhill, which forms a prominent feature of the landscape in the direction of Porthcawl. It has all appearance of a natural phenomenon, since out of the sand, where by all the laws of Nature there should be no trees, a fine clump of trees nevertheless persist in growing. The explanation apparently is that the trees grew first and the sand was blown afterwards in such quantities as entirely to obliterate the soil underneath. That at least is the story as it is told to me.

The course, as I said, has some of the features of down-

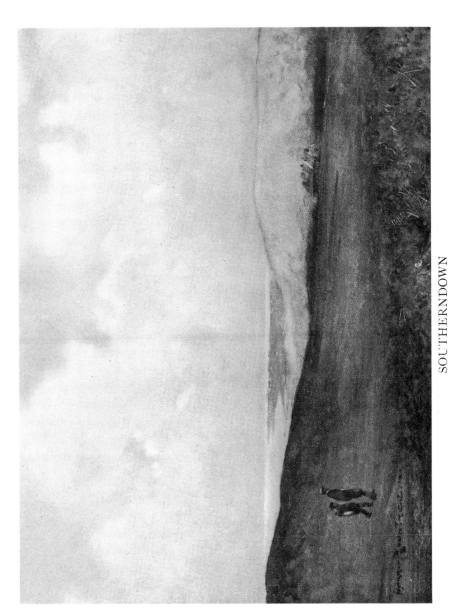

SOUTHERNDOWN

Looking to the last green

land courses, but there is one that it mercifully lacks, namely, those detestable greens which are cut out of the sides of steep hills, and so have a back wall on one side and a sheer drop on the other. The greens at Southerndown are for the most part thoroughly natural in character, and their slopes and undulations are not unduly exaggerated. Another point wherein the course entirely differs from others on the downs is to be found in the presence of bracken, which traps the wandering driver at the sides of the course, and, in the summer at any rate, punishes him with commendable severity.

Three good two-shot holes begin the course : the second and third being particularly testing, so that three fours is perhaps a little too good to expect. Then at the fourth comes our first chance of a three. This is a good and difficult short hole, and deserves some particular description. It is 170 yards long, and the ground slopes fairly briskly from right to left. That being so, one's first instinct would be to play well out to the right and trust to the ball scrambling and kicking down on to the green. This simple little plan has, however, been frustrated by the making of the bunker of the right-hand side. Therefore, we must not push the ball to the right for fear of the bunker, and we must clearly not pull it to the left, lest it run down a steep place away from the green and into troublous country into the bargain. There is nothing for it but to hit the ball quite straight, or, if we want to make the game unnecessarily difficult for ourselves, here is a good chance for trying a 'master-shot.'

GOLF COURSES

Another short hole on the way out, though hardly such a good one, is the eighth; we have to play a typical downland hole, jumping from hillside to hillside over a gully. It is one of those shots that is entirely perplexing to the stranger, who finds the distance almost impossible to judge correctly. At one time the green lay far down at the bottom of the very deepest part of the gully, but that had to be abandoned. To get the ball down was easy enough, but to get it up the hill again was, on a hot day, too tremendous a task, and so the climb has now been made less exhausting by playing only across the shallower part of the ravine. The ninth is a fine two-shotter, where we must hit a high ball from the tee in order to carry a big bunker cut out of the face of a hill; and then, after two comparatively uneventful holes, we come to a third short hole, the twelfth. It is only 130 yards long, but it is not in the least easy for all that. The green is of the island type, surrounded by a generous profusion of bunkers, and the fact that there is usually a fine high wind blowing makes the iron shot a sufficiently difficult one, short though it be.

The thirteenth, a 'dog-leg' hole, is one of the best on the course, where we have to play carefully for position from the tee and must avoid some heavy bracken and thick long grass. The green, too, is well guarded and full of excellent undulations. The fifteenth brings us right up to the club-house, and there is some temptation to curtail the round and fall a victim to lunch, especially as the sixteenth takes in the length of two full drives up a hill

WALES

and directly away from the club. At the seventeenth we get a most lovely view and a four for the hole, if we play two good shots, and then an easy drive and pitch down a flattering hill brings us safely home.

INDEX.

INDEX

INDEX

INDEX

INDEX

GLASGOW : PRINTED AT THE UNIVERSITY PRESS BY ROBERT MACLEHOSE AND CO. LTD.

Afterword
by
Ben Crenshaw

Afterword

One can open a book of Bernard Darwin's to any page, find any line, and be entertained by it. To me, this is the most fascinating quality about his writing—his ability to make each line so good. Can you imagine anyone else writing this well? Here, for example, is a passage I found at random in "The Golf Courses of the British Isles":

"There is a canal, a nasty, insidious serpentine beast of a canal, which winds its way along the left-hand side of the course, and it is our duty, in order to gain distance, to hug it as close as we dare; yet if we show ourselves the least bit too affectionate towards it, this ungrateful canal will assuredly engulf our ball to our utter destruction."

Then there is the scope of the book itself, the describing of all the important courses in England, Scotland, Ireland, and Wales, and the painting of each by Harry Rountree. There is no other golf book like it—the combination of the quality of the writing and the quality of the illustrations is beyond anything that has ever been done.

I have often wondered how such a book came into being, and how Darwin and Rountree collaborated. I have imagined them, like a small band of travellers, scurrying around the countryside—by train in those days—to the different courses. In all probability, given the demands of their careers, they would have been able to arrange only a few excursions together.

One of Rountree's watercolors is of a course called Royal Worlington, near Cambridge University, where Darwin captained the golf team. The painting, on page 154, shows a man standing in the woods glaring at his caddie and his predicament—his ball is lodged behind a tree. If I am not mistaken, this is a portrait of Darwin. It suggests that Darwin and Rountree made at least this one trip together.

Darwin would have discussed with Rountree the courses he knew so well, and he would have pointed out the features of those courses that were of particular fame or merit. Darwin, who was thirty-five when this, his first book, was published, was a very experienced and accomplished golfer and had won some significant amateur events. He had also established himself as a golf writer. In 1908 he began to cover golf for the Times of London *and, in short order, had transformed golf reporting from a recitation of names and numbers into literary sports journalism.*

Harry Rountree, who played golf but not at Darwin's level, was born in Aukland, New Zealand, in 1878. He moved to London shortly before he began his work with Darwin on "The Golf Courses of the British Isles". His task of familiarizing himself with all the courses he intended to paint must have been a monumental one. He became well known as an illustrator of magazines and books. His forte was his drawings of animals, which he did with a keen eye for humorous details. This is evident in his marvelous rendering of the horse taking golfers home from Portmarnock on page 222.

I have three Rountree originals: one oil and two watercolors, neither of which is the original of any of the reproductions in the book. If someone has any of them, I hope they will hold onto these great works. More than likely, the originals are spread among his friends and acquaintances in and near the small town of St. Ives in

Cornwall, where he lived and died in 1950. Evidently, his distinctive, somewhat "fin-de-siecle" style of drawing went out of fashion, and he died in relative obscurity and poverty.

Rountree certainly did his work on the spot. When he arrived at a course, he would select a viewpoint that Darwin had suggested or that appealed to his artistic sense. I believe he had an overall design in mind for his sixty-four watercolors and went out of his way not to repeat himself.

Sometimes Rountree would see a lady walking her child or a group of sheep and include them in the picture. Whenever the opportunity presented itself, he painted in trains, boats, birds, dogs, buildings, people—whatever would help humanize the landscape and bring it to life. His skies were important and they were British skies.

Like the impressionists, Rountree was interested most of all in light and color. In America it's so bright so much of the time that the colors of the courses appear harsher than they do in Great Britain. Where in America do you get those purples and so many different shades of brown, green, and blue? When you look at a Rountree painting, you can only be in Scotland, England, or Ireland.

Occasionally, I am sure, Rountree's renderings must have puzzled Darwin, the quintessential avid golfer. If you look at the wonderful watercolor of the South America hole at Carnoustie (p. 178), a hole admired by Darwin, it is the one hole on the course that doesn't look Scottish. The painting is alive because of the train and the little brook running in front of the green and the farm nearby—but it doesn't look like a links hole, and I can imagine Darwin shaking his head and grumbling at this one. Similarly, the painting of the famous Alps hole at Prestwick shows a perspective that is artistically satisfying but, in golfing terms, hard to decipher. There was nothing that Darwin loved more than an exciting golf hole, and the Alps was one of his favorites—he called it the best blind hole in the world. His reaction to Rountree's watercolor might have been: "Well, Harry, you got the wrong angle there, but it's the Alps all right, and it will have to do."

I also wondered what Darwin's reaction would have been to Rountree's magnificent painting of the town of St. Andrews at sunset as seen from the fifteenth tee (p. 166). Darwin might have wanted him to move to the sixteenth or seventeenth hole where he could have included the clubhouse of the Royal and Ancient. But Rountree may have preferred the primitive, medieval look he achieved, and he might have answered Darwin: "Painting that clubhouse has been done to death."

It was on the thirteenth hole at St. Andrews a few years ago that a very funny but enlightening incident took place. Darwin discusses in "The Golf Courses of the British Isles" the impact of the new rubber-cored ball on the game and the courses. This ball, also known as the Haskell after the Cleveland golfer who invented it, Coburn Haskell, came into play in the early 1900s. Few revolutions in golf proved as sweeping, for the Haskell flew farther through the air than the gutty and rolled much farther on the ground. Both Darwin and Vardon preferred the gutta-percha ball. With it, they felt, golf *was more of an art. But the elastic, rubber-cored ball ushered in the long, modern game we have today.*

The incident I refer to was an attempt to duplicate what it was like to play golf with the gutty. Laurie Auchterlonie, the long-time professional to the Royal and Ancient Golf Club, brought out to the thirteenth tee of the Old Course some new gutties he had just made in his shop. Dressed in jacket, tie, and knickers, Laurie made sand tees for our group, which included myself and Jack Nicklaus, and he handed us our old-fashioned, long-nosed clubs. I drove first, made a good swing, and hit the gutty 190 yards. There was a slight wind in our face. With a wind from our backs the gutty, because it was so light a ball, would have flown much farther, but without a tail wind my guess is that a drive of 200 yards was very respectable. In any case, I was nowhere near the thirteenth green in two shots. The thirteenth is a 425 yard par 4. In the days of the gutty it would have played like a good, solid par 5.

It was Jack's turn. Jack, as you are well aware, is one of the longest drivers in the history of the game. His club slid under the gutty, and the result was a high, little lob that couldn't have travelled more than 20 yards. He took a spoon and tried to get the gutty airborne, but it just rolled over and died, and Jack said: "There's something wrong with this ball". Laurie, perhaps exaggerating his Scots brogue, said: "Ah, Jack, you're just a bloody hacker. You've cut the gutty. You've hit it on the top of your club—no, no, it won't fly now."

Golf was an art with the gutty. It was almost like playing with a ping-pong ball—it was almost that light, even though its shell was hard. You could make the gutty do all sorts of tricks—work it left and right and move it up and down, and you could make it fall absolutely lifeless on the green. No wonder people got so worked up when the rubber-cored ball arrived. It changed the game. I think the rubber-cored ball made the run-up shot easier but, in other respects, you could do far less with it than with the gutty.

If you look at the frontispiece to "The Golf Courses of the British Isles", you will see Rountree's extraordinary painting "Looking Back from the Twelfth Green" with all the links-style bunkers that a player doesn't see when he is playing the hole. However, this explains one of the singular fascinations about St. Andrews, which Darwin brings out: the bunkers are often placed where good drives ought to go. In the background of this painting you can make out golfers on the eleventh green and those two famous bunkers, Hill on the left and Strath on the right. What a golf hole! It may be the best hole in the world, and it's awfully difficult for an architect to adapt. Charles B. Macdonald tried his hand at recreating the Old Course's eleventh, a par 3 of 172 yards, in his thirteenth at the National Golf Links in Southampton, Long Island, generally regarded as the first great American golf course. I played there when the U.S. Open was held in 1986 at neighboring Shinnecock, and I was told that Macdonald's thirteenth green used to extend much farther to the right. If that was the case, it would have made it a better hole and a more successful adaptation, because it would have provided another way to play the hole and a more exciting, dangerous route to the pin.

This is one of the purposes of strategic design—providing golfers with more than one way to play a hole, even a par 3.

The concepts of strategic design were second nature to Darwin and, in a sense, "The Golf Courses of the British Isles" is a textbook of this approach to golf course architecture. His description of the first hole at Hoylake is a classic example of this. I have played Hoylake only once, but I remember many of the holes vividly. Hoylake, of course, is a very famous links. It inaugurated the British Amateur championship in 1885 and, in 1921, it arranged the first amateur international between the United States and Great Britain, which the following year became the Walker Cup. Hoylake, officially the Royal Liverpool Golf Club, was the home course of two of the great amateurs of all time, John Ball and Harold Hilton. The first hole, as Darwin describes it, is a long par 4 which doglegs to the right rather sharply and has a cop—a grassy mound—running the length of the hole along its right side. The cop divides the first fairway from the practice field, which at Hoylake serves as an out-of-bounds hazard for three of its holes. The best way to play the hole is to place your tee-shot as close to the cop as you dare, because this gives you a much shorter second shot as well as the best angle into the green. Here is a perfect example of a great strategic hole, where, the closer you flirt with the trouble, the greater advantage you gain. Every serious study or article on golf-course architecture all the way back to Old Tom Morris has grasped the cardinal principles of strategic golf-course design but, strangely enough, these principles are not understood as clearly today.

One reason for this is that modern designers don't give themselves enough room—or are not allotted enough room by the developers—for their layouts. A golf course with different ways to play each hole requires a good deal of land.

Perhaps another reason that Darwin was so convinced of the inherent superiority of strategically designed courses is that safer routes to the green could then be provided for the higher handicap golfers. Darwin was acutely conscious of the right of even the highest handicap golfer, often referred to by Darwin as a "foozler", to enjoy himself, and his only hope of achieving this was to play his golf on the right kind of course.

If you add to the concept of strategic design the concept that the course must appear to be entirely natural (Darwin called this, "the supreme virtue—that of naturalness"), you would then have, according to Darwin, the perfect golf course.

Some modern courses do not get high marks in this regard. When an architect has found a suitable and roomy enough piece of land for his layout, he must study it to see if he can find the holes that are suggested by the terrain. Any hope of originality in design will come only after time, patience, study, and intimate familiarity with the old classic courses, such as those in "The Golf Courses of the British Isles". A few modern designers take on too many projects at the same time. The results are a little like those of mass production. You can't just rush out to one of your courses in a truck and say, "Well, we better use plan B", and then leave. It's not going to work. The land will suggest after a while what you can do to it.

To my mind, if architects don't build natural-looking courses that can be thoroughly enjoyed by golfers of all handicaps, there's little purpose to golf. What's the magnet that is attracting so many new golfers if it's not the enjoyment of the game? I'm afraid of what some of our modern courses must be doing to our junior golfers. You take a youngster and, if he can't have any kind of fun on a golf course, his interest will be diverted from golf, and he will go on to something else.

I grew up on a Perry Maxwell course, the old Austin Country Club in Austin, Texas. It was a fine course, but it may not be there much longer. A new Austin Country Club course has been built because people thought the old course was in the wrong part of town. It's very sad. I get the same feeling when I read Darwin's description in "The Golf Courses of the British Isles" of Musselburgh, a nine-hole course as famous as a course can be, that, along with Prestwick and St. Andrews, formed the original rota for the British Open championship. Musselburgh, like the old Austin Country Club, is in the wrong part of town. Here is a portion of Darwin's description:

> *"The way to Musselburgh lies for the most part through factory chimneys and slag heaps, nor is the first glimpse of the course much more prepossessing than the surrounding scenery. It looks like an ordinary common on the outskirts of a town, rather flat, and devoid of features, rather hard and rough, not unlike in character that blank stretch of turf at St. Andrews which lies between the clubhouse and the burn. Yet if, after we have played over the course, we*

adhere to this our first view, we shall show ourselves to be persons of superficial minds and of little discernment. It is true that there are comparatively few hazards, and that we ought, therefore, not to get into many of them; but, at the same time, it will gradually dawn upon us that nearly every hole has a governing hazard, to which we must pay due regard—one that will direct our policy for us whether we like it or not . . . of these nine, the first three are as good holes as you can desire to meet anywhere . . ."

Musselburgh lies in the middle of a racetrack today. When I went to look at it, I received the clear impression that quite a few people wanted it ploughed under. In Scotland no less!

Of course, if people would read "The Golf Courses of the British Isles" and absorb what Darwin was saying, there would exist a different attitude about the need to preserve the wonderful old golf courses. Some of them, for example, could be converted into exemplary municipal courses, which we badly need.

Nothing stimulated Darwin more than a good hole. I love the way he takes a hole and, in effect, breaks it down and shows you how it works. He can make you understand why, let's say, a trap in the middle of the fairway is so fascinating or a little semi-blind shot so intriguing. Another of Darwin's qualities as a writer is his ability to put you with him on the hole or the course he is describing. This may be a trite observation, but reading this book is being there. He found a way to humanize golf and golf courses and describe them in ways we can all relate to. He is also honest. If a hole doesn't work, if a course is flawed (this usually means artificial), he will say so. When a friend of his declared that the New Course at St. Andrews was now the second course in

Scotland, by which he meant that it was superior to every other course in Scotland except the Old Course, Darwin's retort was: Not so, what about Prestwick? Even concerning Prestwick—his beloved Prestwick—he will tell you that the new part of the course is not in his judgement perfectly successful because it is not perfectly natural.

If a course is crowded and in general disrepair, it can still have redeeming qualities. This is true of Royal Blackheath, an ancient layout founded in 1608. "Though we may speak flippantly of the bad lies and the numerous hazards on the course, the golf is good golf—far better and more searching than is to be found on many smoothly shaven lawns covered with artificial ramparts." Rountree's watercolor of Blackheath (p. 38) with the caddie marking the line of flight in the midst of a swarming crowd is absolutely perfect. What Darwin said of another course can be applied to Blackheath: every golfer fully expects to be hit on the head by a golf ball at least once a year.

Occasionally, Darwin will describe a course that must represent his ideal—man alone with his thoughts about golf and nature. One of these courses is Sandwich "with its long strip of turf on the way to the seventh hole, that stretches between the sandhills and the sea; a fine spring day, with the larks singing as they seem to sing nowhere else; the sun shining on the waters of Pegwell Bay and lighting up the white cliffs in the distance . . . the extraordinary solitude that surrounds the individual player." A good golf course makes you want to play so badly that you hardly have the patience to change your shoes. Reading "The Golf Courses of the British Isles" *produces the same effect. You want to hop on the next plane and play each and every course described by Darwin and illustrated by Rountree.*

The golf course is, I suppose, the most important aspect of golf, and golf courses can impress people profoundly. What started my interest in the history of the game, the literature and art of golf, and golf course architecture, was playing a great and beautiful course for the first time—The Country Club in Brookline, Massachusetts, in the U.S. Junior Amateur. (In 1988, The Country Club will host the U.S. Open championship on the seventy-fifth anniversary of Ouimet's conquest of Vardon and Ray.) As a raw sixteen year old from Texas playing this course, with its velvet bent grass, opened my eyes to a whole new world, just as going to Scotland, England, or Ireland has for others and, as I fervently hope, reading "The Golf Courses of the British Isles" will for still more of you.

Ben Crenshaw